the *FINAL* choice

d. l. carollo

TATE PUBLISHING, LLC

DEDICATION

This book is dedicated to Archbishop Daniel M. Buechlein, O.S.B., who offered me a spiritual home in the Archdiocese of Indianapolis, and Monsignor Joseph F. Schaedel, Vicar General of the Archdiocese of Indianapolis, who guides and inspires me to trust in Divine Providence.

ACKNOWLEDGMENTS

I am indebted to the following people who encouraged me in my passion to write fiction: Carrie Bellock, for offering sound advice along the way; Mary Ann Wyand, for her editorial assistance; The Missionaries of the Gospel of Life, for their ongoing prayers; and Monsignor Raymond J. Kelly, a priest of the Diocese of Brooklyn, N.Y., for his leadership in the pro-life movement from the beginning.

The Scripture verses are from the *New Oxford Annotated Bible with the Apocrypha, Revised Standard Version*.

PART I—THE PATH CHOSEN

Chapter 1
Pat Marino

Enter by the narrow gate; for the gate is wide and the way is easy, that leads to destruction, and those who enter by it are many. For the gate is narrow and the way is hard, that leads to life, and those who find it are few.
(Matthew 7:13–14)

Friday, December 7

The snow had just begun to fall in New York City early Friday morning. Pat Marino gazed at the powdery mist, already collecting on the ground, from the second-floor bedroom window in her Stuyvesant Town apartment on the Lower East Side of Manhattan. She found it difficult to get out of her bed. She had spent the night tossing, turning and feeling generally miserable. The same virus that had been making the rounds among her co-workers had visited her with a vengeance.

Pat decided to make an all-out effort to throw off the covers and prepare some chamomile tea. As she grabbed her rose-colored flannel robe with its matching satin collar, she glanced in the mirror above her dresser. Her light-brown shoulder-length hair, streaked with blond highlights, needed a good brushing. Around her dark green eyes, there was smeared mascara that she had been too tired and too sick to remove the night before.

"I look like death warmed over," Pat realized.

She slipped into her furry pink slippers. An intense coldness seemed to envelope her as she passed through the living room.

Once in the kitchen, she felt a second blast of cold air. Turning around, she peered out the kitchen window that faced the black wrought-iron gates leading into the parking lot of Immaculate Heart of Mary Church on 14th Street. She spotted Mr. Kim, the owner of the vegetable store next to the parking lot. Today the outside vegetable stands were covered with thick plastic due to the snow. He was bundled up in his hooded down jacket, scarf and gloves.

Moving away from the window, she stared at her yellow striped kitchen curtains. They were still; there was no draft. She glanced at the wall thermometer. It registered 71 degrees.

"Why do I feel so cold in here? Must be a fever," she thought.

Putting the kettle on to boil, Pat walked back into the living room. She gathered the bills and junk mail stacked on her antique mahogany desk in the corner of her otherwise modern living room. Throwing half the mail away, she decided to sink into her favorite black leather recliner.

Pushing the side lever back, she raised her legs. It took all her effort. She continued to shiver.

Something was unnatural and terrible about this cold. It was getting to her. Relaxing in the chair, she closed her eyes as the room began to revolve around her. She felt sick to her stomach. Moments latter, as the dizziness and nausea passed, Pat's mind wandered back to the cold winter day, four years earlier, when she moved out of her family home in Sheepshead Bay into her Stuyvesant apartment. With her first few paychecks secured from her underwriting job, she began her life of independence.

Pat was delighted to be emancipated from her parents' archaic rules and regulations, including weekly attendance at Sunday Mass. Despite the fact that she currently lived directly across the street from a Catholic church, her shadow never crossed its threshold.

Though she loved Dominic and Louise Marino, they were definitely "old school" and out of touch with the times. Given her parents' values, she hid from them not only her absence from Sunday Mass, but also her budding relationship with Paul Murphy, who had temporarily moved in with her while he was in between jobs.

Dominic Marino and Louise Amato grew up in Bensonhurst, Brooklyn, just doors away from each other. Though five generations from the Marino and Amato families could claim American citizenship, Pat considered them foreigners to American soil. More precisely, she considered them aliens to the planet Earth. Often, when her parents preached sermons to her on the values of family, faith and hard work, Pat would amuse herself by pretending they were speaking an alien language. It took her mind off the content of their sermons. She would often hear her mother say, "Pat, you're giving us that strange look again. Are you listening to us?"

Pat had not thought about Paul for a long time. She preferred it that way. He was securely placed in the inactive file of her mind. Though he once was the man she wished to marry, she later realized that she had fallen in love with an image of the man, and not with the actual man.

Pondering her relationship with Paul, Pat realized that she had never brought Paul home to meet her parents before or after he moved in with her. She met Paul through mutual friends at an informal gathering, and was flattered by the attention he paid her. He was a real charmer. He worked as a physical education instructor at Lafayette High School in Brooklyn. He was naturally athletic and competitive, and had dreams of joining a professional football team after graduating from St. Vincent's University. But severe injuries to his right knee and ankle destroyed all hope for a professional career in sports after college.

Paul asked Pat out numerous times. Their dates were built around attending some sporting event followed by a late lunch or dinner. Within months, Paul introduced

Pat to mountain climbing, scuba diving and snow skiing. He brought excitement and adventure into her otherwise boring life.

One weekend in December, Pat went with Paul and some of their friends to Colorado for a ski weekend. It was during that time that she became pregnant. Two months later, Pat took an over-the-counter pregnancy test. She tested herself a second time. Again, the results were positive. She approached Paul with the news.

"You're what? I thought you were on the pill."

"I was, but I may have forgotten to take them several days last month. Remember how I was on antibiotics and felt lousy? My stomach was upset and it must have slipped my mind."

"Slipped your mind?"

Paul ran his hands through his curly red hair. His baby blue eyes glared at her.

Then, sarcastically, he added, "A grocery item may slip your mind, but this . . . ? I don't want the baby. Get an abortion."

His words seared her mind and heart.

"An abortion?"

"Yeah, an abortion. I'll pay for it."

"I want this baby, Paul!"

"Pat, read my lips. No baby, not now. I'm not ready to settle down. I told you that. You know what you have to do! There's nothing to discuss here."

Seeing how upset she was, Paul tried to soften his approach.

Pat could barely comprehend his words or look at him.

"I don't want an abortion," she whispered as she held back tears.

"Having this baby is not an option," he told her.

Paul grabbed his jacket in anger and walked out of their apartment. He returned very late that night and reeked of liquor. Pat pretended to be asleep.

The next day, she sat immobile on her brown over-stuffed corduroy couch with the cell phone in her lap. Next to her was the Manhattan telephone directory. She looked under "Abortions" and found several clinics in the metropolitan area. Finally, she called one clinic and made the necessary arrangements for a Saturday morning procedure, knowing that Paul had issued an ultimatum and wouldn't change his mind. Making the appointment seemed to drain her of all her energy.

The day of the abortion, Paul drove her to the Women's Reproductive Health Center in Manhattan. The clinic was located in what appeared to be an ordinary office building. She didn't want anyone to know she was having an abortion. The multipurpose building concealed the true reason many women entered it during office hours. An insurance agency, real estate brokers, lawyers and even hairstylists on the ground floor shared prime space with the Reproductive Health Center Inc.

"You're doing the right thing for us, Pat. I'll pick you up in a few hours. You'll be fine in a few days."

Paul leaned over to kiss her. She moved away from him.

"Aren't you coming in, Paul?"

"It's hard to park around here. Anyway, there's no point just sitting around in there."

Pat slammed the car door as she walked toward the clinic. She could see some sidewalk counselors walking toward her. She glanced at the graphic photos of aborted babies.

"Get the hell away from me, all of you!" she shouted. She wondered how they knew she was going in for an abortion.

Once inside the building, Pat walked briskly to the elevator and pushed the button for the fourth floor, where the abortion clinic was located. The place reminded her of a dentist's office. There were many more rooms beyond the reception area, which were clean and neat. Colorful pastel prints of flowers were strategically placed on the walls. She detested them.

She filled out the necessary paperwork for the receptionist then kept to herself. Paul wanted her to pay cash for the abortion. As she handed over the money, she felt anger.

Taking her seat, she ignored the other women in the waiting room by focusing her attention on an outdated issue of *Time* magazine. She did look up and noticed an African-American woman, who was visibly upset after being told that the ultrasound revealed twins. Of course, the price for the procedure was doubled.

Though some of the women were talking to each other, including the African-American with the twins, Pat had no intention of communicating with anyone. She wanted to get the procedure over with as quickly as possible and get on with her life. She noticed that there were fourteen women and only two men in the room. Perhaps these women also had boyfriends or husbands who found the parking too difficult, and would return in a few hours after it was all over.

Pat couldn't recall anything she read in the magazine. She didn't remember the clinic staff or the physician who performed her abortion. The details she remembered with clarity were the pictures of the aborted fetuses outside the building, the number of people in the waiting room, the woman with the twins, and the bleeding and cramping she experienced the following day. The whole morning in the clinic was a surreal event in her life.

Before she left the clinic, she called a taxi service to pick her up and take her home. After she dialed Paul's cell phone, she listened to his recorded message. "You've reached Paul. This certainly is your lucky day! Leave your name, a brief message and, depending on who you are, I may or may not return your call."

"What a lousy message," she thought.

Pat realized that his message was quite consistent with his personality. If Paul liked you, he would charm you. If he disliked you or had no immediate use for you, he simply blew you off like a speck of dust. Pat waited for the beep.

"I have a ride. Don't inconvenience yourself."

Pat left the abortion clinic feeling numb. She walked past the sidewalk counselors, who expressed genuine concern for her well-being.

As she opened the door of the taxi, she heard one of the younger women say, "I had an abortion several years ago. I'll pray for you."

Pat instinctively turned around to the woman to thank her, but stopped short of responding. She got into the back seat of the taxi and watched as the foreign-born driver from Africa skillfully weaved the car in and out of traffic as though it were nothing more than an obstacle course. She was conscious that the procedure had done something to her.

With each passing day, the numbness Pat felt was replaced by increasing anger and resentment toward Paul. How could someone she loved do this to her? How could he ask her to destroy their child? Worst of all, how could she allow herself to do it? Often, she would reassure herself that she made the best decision under the worst of circumstances.

"It's not fair to bring an unwanted child into the world. I made the best choice."

Within a month of her abortion, Paul moved out of the apartment and out of Pat's life forever. He never understood Pat's change of attitude toward him. He dismissed her abortion as something that was unfortunate but necessary. Their relationship disintegrated in record time.

On the morning Paul left, Pat stood by the apartment door as he wheeled out his last suitcase. They exchanged no bitter words, no angry words; there were no significant words at all. There was only a thick silence that you could have cut with a knife. The abortion had been their final topic of discussion. It had left her in silent anger. Paul was simply left speechless.

Suddenly, the doorbell rang and Pat was brought back to the present. She grabbed the brown and beige afghan she had thrown on her couch and wrapped it around herself. She couldn't stop shivering. She walked clumsily over to her apartment door.

As Pat reached the door, she stumbled several times. Grabbing the doorknob, she lost her balance as the buzzer startled her. For a split second, she felt very disoriented and dizzy. Then, regaining her balance, she looked through the peephole. It was her neighbor, Eileen Fitzpatrick.

"Hi Pat. I just wanted to come by and offer you some bundt cake I made the other day. I'm leaving for Florida tomorrow morning and staying with my sister, Betsy, in Naples. I can't take this cold weather anymore! But I can come back later. It seems as though I caught you at a bad time."

Mrs. Fitzpatrick was a tall slender woman in her early seventies. Her white hair was always attractively styled by her youngest daughter, Patrice, who owned her own beauty salon on Long Island. Her wardrobe consisted of a wide array of fine suits and dresses that she had collected through the years. They were timeless in their elegance. The clothes fit the woman in Pat's estimation. Mrs. Fitzpatrick was one classy lady.

Feeling the warmth of the afghan around her, Pat protested.

"Oh, no, Mrs. Fitzpatrick. Please, come in. Thank you for thinking of me."

The sound of the kettle whistling interrupted Pat's next sentence.

"Let me turn off the kettle."

"I'll have some tea with you, if you're offering!" said Mrs. Fitzpatrick.

"Sure. Tell me about Florida," Pat added as she started to walk back toward the kitchen.

"Oh, Pat, I can't stay very long. My daughter, Beverly, is on her way to take me to the eye doctor's office. My cataract surgery went very well and now I need a new prescription for glasses. She'll be here shortly."

Pat smiled slightly, knowing that Mrs. Fitzpatrick's short visits could turn out to be very long. But she liked the old woman who went out of her way for everyone, even for Pat.

While growing up in Sheepshead Bay, Eileen Fitzpatrick and her own mother were teachers in the neighborhood Catholic school. Mrs. Fitzpatrick had taught Pat in the fourth-grade. Pat had many fond memories of "Mrs. Fitz," as her classmates affectionately called her.

What especially appealed to the students was how Mrs. Fitzpatrick always shared amusing stories about her four children and her husband, who was deceased. She was widowed fairly young, in her early fifties, but always wore her wedding and engagement rings. She referred to her husband as "Mr. Fitzpatrick, God rest his soul." As a child, Pat always thought that "God rest his soul" was part of his official name or title.

"Make yourself comfortable in the living room." While pouring water into the cups, Pat recalled how Mrs. Fitzpatrick comforted her after Paul moved out. She didn't judge Pat, but she did, in no uncertain terms, recommend that Pat return to the practice of her Catholic faith and a healthier attitude toward marriage.

"Honey, these relationships don't last. In the end, you'll only feel used. Marriage may be old-fashioned, but it was God who fashioned it. I like to think God knows best."

Pat returned to the living room a moment later. Mrs. Fitzpatrick was gone, and so was her bundt cake.

"Where on earth did she go?" Pat wondered.

Afghan and all, she ventured into the hallway. Mrs. Fitzpatrick lived in the apartment next door. She knocked on her neighbor's door, but there was no answer.

Returning to her living room, Pat called Mrs. Fitzpatrick's number. There was no answer. As Mrs. Fitzpatrick's voice mail recording came on, she said, "Hey, Mrs. Fitz. You disappeared! Are you O.K.? Give me a buzz. You probably didn't hear your door bell."

The cup of tea warmed Pat as she wondered about the episodes of cold in her apartment and about Mrs. Fitzpatrick's quick departure.

CHAPTER 2
JAY ROKER

Do not lay up for yourselves treasures on earth, where moth and rust consume and where thieves break in and steal, but lay up for yourselves treasures in heaven, where neither moth nor rust consumes and where thieves do not break in and steal. For where your treasure is, there will your heart be also.

(Matthew 6:19–21)

Jay Roker sat in his parked car. It was freezing cold. The snow was lightly covering the ground in Jackson Heights, Queens. He glanced at his wristwatch. It was twenty after eleven in the morning. He had taken a personal day from work. The mechanic's shop was to be his first stop. That "check engine" warning kept lighting up.

Shifting into reverse, he took his foot off the brake, but the car went dead. Putting his Eagle Jeep into park, he tried again and again to restart it. Taking the keys out of the ignition, Jay began to formulate a plan. He'd have to find someone willing to jumpstart his car so he could drive it to the garage for repair. Maybe, with a little luck, the auto club could get a tow-truck to him within the hour. He needed to get to a phone.

Living in Jackson Heights meant having to park several blocks from his apartment. If he was lucky, he didn't have to catch a bus to his parked car. He had left his cell phone on the coffee table in his apartment. The closest phone was across the street at the corner convenience store. Frustrated, Jay opened the driver's side of the car without even looking into his side mirror.

Suddenly, a car careened to the left to avoid hitting him.

"Wow, was that a close call!"

Feeling extremely foolish and quite dazed, he began walking briskly to the convenience store. There was an unusual coldness that seemed to penetrate his short black leather jacket and his jeans. His feet felt numb in his brown cowboy boots that desperately needed a good shine. He lifted his collar to shield himself from the cold and the snow that was falling steadily then he buried his hands deep into his jacket pockets.

Jay was tall and muscular. He liked to work out at the gym a few times a week. He bore a striking resemblance to actor Denzel Washington.

"Forget about looking like the dude. I wish I just had his money," he often said to those who noticed the resemblance.

Jay lamented the fact that he had to work as a security guard, and had to stand outside a building braving the elements, day in and day out, for a miserable salary and benefits.

He intended to interview for several managerial positions at various department stores in Manhattan. After all, he majored in Business at Queens College, though he never did complete his sophomore year. All those credits certainly had to be worth something in the real world.

"Jackson, you never finish what you start. Boy, you'll never amount to anything if you leave everything half done!" his Grandma Pearl used to say to him.

Jay looked up into the heavens.

"Well, Grandma, maybe this time you'll be wrong. I think they'll see I'm the man they want."

The Roker family once resided in the Fort Greene section of Brooklyn. This area near the Navy Yard was as dangerous as any battlefield. The residents didn't have to worry about landmines or missiles, but they did have to worry about drug dealers and violent criminals. The towering housing projects for low-income families produced many casualties. Among the casualties were his parents.

When he was 10 years old, Jay's father, Jamil, started smoking crack and easily became addicted. Within a year, he lost his trucking job and his life. His body was found badly decomposed in an abandoned building in East New York, Brooklyn, several weeks after he was reported missing.

Sondra, Jamil's common-law wife and Jay's mother, found herself alone with three children to raise and felt overwhelmed. She turned to her parents, Claude and Pearl Kelley. By pooling their resources, Sondra, Pearl and Claude Kelley bought a house in Jackson Heights, Queens, where Jay and his sisters enjoyed the benefits of extended family living.

Through the years, Jay's grandparents struggled with the upbringing of their grandchildren in an environment that was so hostile to their traditional Christian values. Growing up in the backwoods of Alabama did not prepare Grandma Pearl or Claude for the bumpy ride of rearing youth in an urban area. There were times they wanted the whole family to move back down south where the simple life would provide more sanity. However, Sondra and her children would remind them that there was nothing for them in the backwoods except lives of poverty.

As Jay walked toward the store, he noticed that there was an uncanny stillness; nothing was moving. Moments before, there were cars, buses and people in motion. Now, there was only an eerie silence and stillness, plus the terrible freezing cold air that made him shiver.

The traffic lights were not functioning. But since no cars were to be seen, Jay crossed the street with no problem.

"Gee, this street would have been impossible to cross just five minutes ago."

All the stores appeared empty and dark. He walked into Marty Cohen's store. No one was at the register and no one appeared to be in the store.

Jay called out to the storeowner.

"Hey, Marty, I want to buy a lottery ticket."

"I'll be with you in just a minute."

Relieved to hear Marty's voice, Jay relaxed.

"Might as well buy a newspaper, too," thought Jay.

Finally, Marty emerged, smiling.

"How can I help you?" he asked.

"What happened to all the lights? Where is everyone?" asked Jay.

"I'm not aware of any power shortages. Listen, I can't sell you a lottery ticket right now. The machine is malfunctioning."

"Well, here's the change for a newspaper. I'll stop by later to buy the winning ticket. I'll need the money to pay for my car repairs."

Glancing over at the wall, he noticed a sign stating that the phone was out of order. Annoyed, Jay picked up the paper and left the store.

The traffic lights were working again. Cars were moving, and a bus passed by as he took a deep breath and looked both ways before crossing against the light. Looking down at the newspaper, he noticed that it had the date for the previous day, Thursday, December 6. Turning around, he crossed the street and walked back to the store. Instead of Marty at the register, his wife, Libby, greeted him.

"Libby, your husband just sold me yesterday's paper a few minutes ago," Jay chided her.

"Stop kidding, Jay. Marty isn't here. He had to fly out to Philadelphia to see his father. They think he had a stroke or something. I've been here the whole time."

"Sorry to hear that."

He hesitated to say anything more to Libby about his encounter with Marty. Jay looked around the store, trying to spot Marty.

"Just take another paper," she said.

As Libby gestured to the pile of newspapers, several people walked in to buy lottery tickets. Jay was amazed to see Libby enter the numbers in the machine with no problem.

Jay picked up his newspaper and exited the store.

"Gee, these headlines seem familiar."

Looking up at the yellow traffic light, Jay was sure he had seen Marty. He was sure he had asked for a lottery ticket and was told the machine wasn't working. Jay shook his head.

"I still have to find a pay phone. Maybe I'm going nuts."

Returning to his vehicle, Jay sat in the front seat, trying to get warm before planning his strategy to find a functioning pay phone. He lowered the sun visor and removed the picture of his mother, his grandmother and his sisters, Sharelle and Shana. The photo had been taken the year he lost his Grandma Pearl. His grandfather had already passed away years before.

He laughed aloud as he thought of his grandmother and her gentile southern ways. She always taught Jay and his sisters to say "Yes, Ma'am" and "No, Sir" when addressing their elders. He missed his old-fashioned grandmother, who was a kind and gentle soul.

Fumbling for still another photo in the visor, he found a picture of his nephew, Duane. Sharelle, his mother, was holding him in her arms. The picture had been taken as Duane was throwing a kiss to Jay.

Jay laughed aloud and made a mental note that he wanted to buy Duane a new bicycle for his upcoming fourth birthday.

"Buddy, you almost didn't make it into this world! I'm going to make sure every one of your birthdays is special."

Then Jay felt guilt and shame because he knew he had not fought for the life of his nephew when it counted.

CHAPTER 3
DR. SAMUEL WEISS

The eye is the lamp of the body. So, if your eye is sound, your whole body will be full of light; but if your eye is not sound, your whole body will be full of darkness. If then the light in you is darkness, how great is the darkness!
(Matthew 6:22–23)

Dr. Samuel Weiss slammed the door of his highly polished gray Cadillac. He walked around to the door leading from his garage to his kitchen in his upscale Westchester, New York, Tudor-style home. The alarm system was activated, and he began to enter the code to disarm it. He was distracted as he searched for the keys in his pocket.

Like his Cadillac, Sam was big. Standing six feet tall and being overweight, he often joked that he needed to be just a few inches taller so that his weight could be more evenly distributed.

Sam felt a sharp pain at the back of his head.

"I'll have to take something for this lousy headache."

He brought his hand to the back of his head. Except for a border of curly white hair around his head, Sam was bald.

Years earlier, he had purchased a very expensive toupee. Ethel, his wife of thirty-nine years, was already in bed reading one of her mystery novels. She looked up from her book as Sam walked into the room with his new toupee.

In her usual melodramatic style, she yelled, "Sammy, hurry! Hurry! There's a man in our bedroom impersonating you, and he has something dead on top of his head."

They both had a good laugh. Sam placed the toupee in its special box. It never was to be seen again. On special occasions, when he wore his yarmulke, his baldness was covered up very nicely.

"Too bad I'm not a religious Jew!"

Sam's father, Sol, however, was a religious Jew. He was a decent man who worked hard all his life to provide for his family. He was so proud of Sam when he became the head of Obstetrics at University Hospital in New York early on in his career. He bragged to his friends about Sam the doctor, Jacob the lawyer and Rachel the teacher. His three children made him proud because of their accomplishments. His fourth son, Bernard, was retarded. He never referred to Bernie's professional accomplishments in life. Sol would simply say that Bernie knew how to give you a million-dollar smile and priceless hug.

Bernie grew up loved and nurtured in the Weiss household. He had the mentality of a 6-year-old, and, like any child, he had his good and bad days. But for Sol and Sarah Weiss, the days with Bernie were good ones. Bernie enjoyed his simple life collecting baseball cards because all the kids on the block collected them. He carried his own blue rabbit's foot with a key to the front door. It was as though he was given the key to the city. He had learned to lock and unlock their door on his own, and could stay in front of the house for periods of time unattended. Bernie's simple life ended from heart complications at the age of 22. Their son's death left a vacuum in many hearts, including Sam's.

After his brother's death, Sam, then 30 years old, seriously doubted the existence of God. To the horror of his father and mother, he liked to identify himself as an "agnostic Jew." As a physician, he witnessed life and death, and death left him speechless. God's existence was more of problem for him than a mystery.

As Sam put his key into the lock, it didn't turn. He tried again and again, with no success, to get into his house.

"Well, isn't this great! I'm locked out."

He glanced over and noticed that his wife's white Lexus was parked next to his car.

Lifting his cell phone from his jacket pocket, he tried to call his home number to see if Ethel would pick up the phone. Pressing the button to activate his phone, he noticed that nothing happened.

"Dead. My luck," thought Sam.

He walked back to his car and discovered the doors were securely locked with the car keys dangling from the ignition. Sam regretted not hiding an extra pair of car keys somewhere in the garage. Annoyed, he walked over to the garage door and pressed the button on the wall to open it. Nothing happened.

Feeling trapped, Sam began to think of what he could do to liberate himself from the garage. Looking up through his silver wire eyeglasses that revealed dark brown eyes, he glanced at the small window in the garage which was open several inches.

Unsuccessfully, he attempted to force the window wide open. Ethel must have wanted some fresh air in the garage. Why didn't she just open the garage doors? Maybe she thought she'd set off the security alarm, but the alarm was only wired for the house.

As he eyed the width of the window and his own midriff, he lamented not having committed himself enough to the Atkins Diet. Suddenly, his cell phone beeped on with its familiar noise and the garage door lifted.

"This is like the Twilight Zone!" thought Sam.

He dealt with the phone and garage door. Then, taking his house key out of his pocket, he inserted it into the lock of his door and with ease entered his newly remodeled kitchen. Ethel had outdone herself with the remodeling project. Everything was state- of-the-art technology.

"Maybe now Ethel will start cooking again."

Looking back at the door, Sam shook his head in disbelief.

"Well, I'll be damned if I can explain what just happened!"

He glanced at the thermostat on the kitchen wall. It read 70 degrees, but if felt much colder.

Sam wandered from room to room looking for his wife.

"Ethel. Ethel. I'm home."

There was no response. He strolled into the couple's master bedroom. Everything in the bedroom was furnished in the colonial style. Their king-size bed was covered with an elaborate quilt. The soothing blend of green, orange, brown and beige colors brightened the room. Adding to the warmth of the environment were the light yellow curtains, oak-paneled walls and deep plush beige and brown rug Ethel had selected for the room.

Sam thought about Ethel's talent for interior decorating. Grinning, he tried to project Ethel back to colonial times in America. He laughed heartily as he tried to imagine her fetching water from a well, baking her own bread from scratch or darning his socks by candlelight!

His good humor left him as his eyes fixed on a framed photo displayed on the fireplace mantle. He, Ethel and Helene were posing in front of the castle at Disney World in Florida on their daughter's tenth birthday. They were so happy that day. Helene was wearing her Mouseketeer ears and was radiant with joy.

He reached out to touch the photo, as if to reach back in time to take hold of the moment.

"Yeah, life can throw you some real curve balls!"

Shifting his gaze from the photo, Sam's thoughts returned to Ethel. She was a good wife except for the fact that she spent a little too much money.

A former pediatric nurse, she had committed herself to raising money for worthy medical causes early on in their marriage. For the past fifteen years, she had worked diligently on fundraisers to help find a cure for Lou Gehrig's disease, the worst of the forty or so motor neuron diseases. Her own mother had wasted away from the disease shortly after she and Sam were married. Ethel also raised money for St. Jude Children's Research Hospital in Tennessee, which specialized in research for pediatric cancer and other childhood catastrophic diseases. Her heart was always in the right place.

Like Sam's parents, she was proud of her husband's achievements, especially when he was appointed head of Obstetrics. But she was definitely not in favor of his last decision to open a clinic in Queens that specialized in "reproductive health issues," as he called it. But Sam was firmly committed to his decision, and she knew that her stubborn husband was beyond reason. She once asked him if he would consider listening to her.

"But, Ethel, I always listen to you."

"Sure, Sammy, you listen to me. I listen to the birds, but do I understand what they are saying?"

Realizing that his wife probably had gone to visit the Fletchers next door, Sam decided to go back into the garage and collect the daily newspapers he had left in the car. He removed his blue sports jacket that he had purchased at the Big Man's Shop and loosened his gray and white tie. He picked up a spare set of car keys and headed for the garage. Tired from his day, he just wanted to kick off his shoes, read and relax. When Ethel returned, he would offer to take her out to her favorite Italian restaurant. He knew she would accept his offer.

Chapter 4
Denise Smith

"Why do you call me 'Lord, Lord,' and not do what I tell you? Every one who comes to me and hears my words and does them, I will show you what he is like: he is like a man building a house, who dug deep, and laid the foundation upon rock; and when a flood arose, the stream broke against that house, and could not shake it, because it had been well built. But he who hears and does not do them is like a man who built a house on the ground without a foundation; against which the stream broke, and immediately it fell, and the ruin of that house was great."

(Luke 6:46–49)

Denise Smith was scheduled to terminate her pregnancy the next day, Saturday, December 8, at the Caring Clinic for Women in Jackson Heights, Queens. How could she possibly have this baby? A child was not in their plans. She and her boyfriend, Greg, had a year left at St. Vincent's Law School and marriage was not on the docket. They had a right to their careers, and a chance at success before getting tied down with the responsibilities of parenting.

As Denise passed her mother, Maggie, in the kitchen, she wished she could confess her secret and her fears. Knowing that her mother would insist on her having the baby, Denise could never share her dilemma.

"Denise, is everything O.K.? You've been so distant lately. Is something bothering you?"

"I'm fine, Mom. It's the pressure of school. I'll be down later for dinner. I'll be in my room studying."

Maggie was in her late fifties, petite and attractive. Her short blond hair was neatly styled. Unlike her daughter, she wore no makeup, did not have her nails done and was totally uninterested in clothing and shoes that were not practical or affordable. Her one extravagant act was to put a rinse on her hair to give it a golden shade of blonde. Denise called her mother a "plain Jane." She once convinced her mother to allow one of her friends to style her hair and give her a cosmetic makeover. After viewing the results, her mother simply smiled. She was a good sport. The next day, however, she was back to being a "plain Jane."

As Maggie unloaded the dishwasher, she called back, "Fine, honey. No matter how old you are, I still worry about you!"

Denise climbed the stairway to her bedroom. It hadn't changed since she was 18. It had an adolescent look to it, not the look of a future lawyer. Her eyes wandered to a framed wedding photo on her desk that included all the members of her family. It was taken four years earlier on her older sister's wedding day. Since that time, Debbie, her sister, gave birth to twins and had another child on the way.

"The family is growing," thought Denise.

She felt ambivalent about the decision she had made to terminate her pregnancy.

Looking away from the photo, her eyes found her reflection in the mirror. She was wearing black stretch pants and a genuine beige Irish turtleneck sweater. Despite the sweater, Denise was chilled.

"Must be my nerves."

Her long light blond hair was twisted and pinned up at the back of her head. She stared at her own steel-blue eyes as though she were looking into the eyes of a stranger.

Glancing around her room, she determined that changes were in order.

"I'll have to do something to this room. I'm not a child anymore."

Feeling totally exhausted, she collapsed on her bed and grabbed the stuffed bear that her parents gave her when she was 6 years old. She closed her eyes and remembered the Christmas Eve when she received the stuffed animal as a gift.

The Smith family was gathered around the six-foot Christmas tree. The blinking lights always intrigued Denise. The garland, tinsel and colorful Christmas balls delighted her. At the top of the tree, her father had placed a silver star.

"This is the star of Bethlehem," he reminded his children. "Your mother and I purchased it for our Christmas tree when we were first married."

John Smith was over five feet, ten inches tall and had a very pronounced beer belly. His once brown hair was almost completely white at the age of 61. Denise literally looked up to her father. She, like her mother, barely reached five feet, three inches tall. What Denise recalled, as a child, about her father were his blue overalls.

He was a plumber. Denise loved his overalls and thought it was really neat to have tools hanging from one's side. For the longest time, she wanted to be a plumber, until the day their toilet backed up on the second floor. At the tender age of 9, she decided that wearing overalls wasn't necessarily the coolest thing on Earth.

As Denise looked down at the stuffed bear she received as a little girl, she recalled that, like most children, she was eager to open her presents before the family went to Mass. Only two of her four brothers and sisters were born by that time. She was about 6 years old. Her mother was pregnant and anticipating the baby's arrival in early March.

But instead of a birth that March, the family mourned the loss of a little boy that Maggie miscarried shortly before the New Year.

"Denise, your mother lost the baby today," her father explained. "He won't be coming home from the hospital."

Denise felt cheated. She wondered about the nursery that her parents had prepared for the newest baby. Joshua would never sleep in that room, or see the Christmas tree with the silver star of Bethlehem, or open the gifts that Santa brought on Christmas Eve. It just didn't seem fair to Denise that her baby brother would never come home.

"But he's with God now," said her father. "Someday, we'll all be together in heaven with him."

Suddenly, the alarm next to her bed went off. Denise was startled. She didn't remember falling asleep, but she must have dozed off shortly after she laid down to rest. She looked at the time. It was almost six o'clock. Rubbing her eyes and stretching, she figured that she had set the alarm so she could be out of the house by six-thirty to get to her appointment.

Brenda, her best friend, was going to meet her at the Caring Clinic for Women. Denise knew that Brenda would always be there for her in times of crisis.

"This day is going to be a crisis day, if there was ever one," thought Denise.

Brenda and Denise grew up together. They were more like sisters than friends. In fact, some people mistook them for sisters since they were always together. Brenda had naturally curly strawberry blond hair and green eyes. She was much taller than Denise and was always self-conscious as a child that she had to wear glasses and braces on her teeth. She absolutely hated the freckles that covered her face, arms and legs. As an adult, she changed her glasses to contact lenses and her teeth were now perfectly aligned, but the freckles were as pronounced as ever.

As she prepared to get herself ready, Denise realized that she hadn't had dinner with her family on Friday night. Looking at her cell phone, the date was December 8. It was, in fact, Saturday.

"I'm surprised no one tried to wake me up and tell me it was dinner time."

As she dragged herself out of bed, she noticed a paper that had been slipped under her door. It was a note from her mother.

Denise,

You were sleeping so soundly that I decided not to wake you for dinner. There are leftovers in the refrigerator for you. Mom

"Oh, well. I can't eat anyway. I have to fast before the procedure."

A knot developed in her stomach at the thought of the procedure. Walking over to her bedroom window, Denise glanced across the street. The Hermanns had moved several years ago, and now another little girl occupied Brenda's bedroom.

"Life was so simple back then," thought Denise.

Walking slowly to the bathroom to shower and dress, Denise paused to look down the hallway. She was especially quiet, careful not to wake anyone. The house seemed unusually cold and still. Even the family dog, Lady, a white miniature poodle, didn't budge from her pillow in the hallway when she passed her.

Wearing a navy blue jogging suit, white sneakers and her heavy light-blue ski jacket, Denise opened the front door. As she slipped quietly into the darkness, a blast of cold air penetrated every fiber of her being. She was cold, so very cold.

CHAPTER 5
SHELLEY DeSIMONE

"For no good tree bears bad fruit, nor again does a bad tree bear good fruit; for each tree is known by its own fruit. For figs are not gathered from thorns, nor are grapes picked from a bramble bush. The good man out of the good treasure of his heart produces good, and the evil man out of his evil treasure produces evil; for out of the abundance of the heart his mouth speaks."
(Luke 6:43–45)

Michelle "Shelley" DeSimone, a patent attorney in Indianapolis, tapped her long, manicured Passion Red fingernails on her desk as she waited for Mark Kramer to call her. She expected his call between ten o'clock and ten-fifteen in the morning. He would probably call her from his downtown office in Indianapolis or from his car. Mark had also worked out of his home office in Carmel until he separated from his wife, Laura. He had a booming business renting homes to prospective clients with the option to buy.

She glanced at the street below her downtown office as a steady stream of traffic passed down Capitol Avenue. It was a bright and sunny day. Shelley slipped on her brown blazer in an attempt to get warm. Standing to read the temperature on the wall, she was surprised that it was 72 degrees.

Shelley's cell phone rang. Shifting her short auburn hair away from her ear, she closed her eyes as she heard Mark's voice.

"Shelley, it's me."

"Mark, it's so good to hear your voice."

She gathered her courage.

"Mark, where are you calling from?"

"From my home office."

Shelley began to bite her bottom lip.

"Have you made a decision?"

"Shelley, I'm not divorcing Laura. I have two kids, for God's sake! I don't want to destroy my marriage. It's true that Laura and I were having problems. But we are working things out now. I can't throw away ten years of marriage! Our relationship should never have happened. It needs to end."

The abruptness of Mark's tone and his rehearsed lines pierced Shelley to the heart. She couldn't or wouldn't believe her ears. It was too painful.

"Mark, I love you. I can't imagine my life without you," she answered with a tone of desperation.

"Shelley, you are making this very difficult. I never meant to hurt you. I really thought my marriage was over. Under different circumstances, I could have fallen in love with you."

As she listened to Mark's voice, she could imagine him playing with his pen and repeatedly stroking his brown mustache and beard as they spoke. He tended to fidget a lot when talking on the phone. He had a lot of nervous energy.

Shelley felt the room swirl around her. She didn't want to believe that their relationship was over. She was hoping to be married by her thirtieth birthday the following year. She was hoping to be married to Mark.

"Shelly, Laura and I began marriage counseling three weeks ago. She confronted me and said I had to make a decision about our marriage. She knew I had been unfaithful. She's giving me a second chance. I really want that second chance! Laura is expecting again. I owe it to Laura and to the kids to make this marriage work."

Shelley sat back.

"She's expecting?"

Then she hunched over in her chair.

"Shelley, I don't want to lose my wife and family. She knows that I'm making this call to you."

It was clear that Mark was serious about his marriage. Shelley realized that Mark had never lied to her about their relationship. She had known Mark less than eight months, but didn't date him until he and his wife separated, by mutual agreement. The separation officially ended three weeks ago, perhaps when they went into counseling and he discovered that his wife was pregnant with their child.

Shelley assured Mark that she would not cause him any embarrassment. They wished each other well. As she hung up the phone, she began to sob uncontrollably. But as quickly as the tears came, they stopped. In a trance-like state, she wiped the tears from her eyes and straightened up.

"I thought he was falling in love with me. For him, it was just a fling, an affair!"

Shelley felt humiliated. She wanted Mark to leave his wife for her. She was simply the "other woman" who would be left with nothing.

It seemed her love life was doomed to failure. Before dating Mark, she was in a relationship with George McCue, Esquire. This was another dismal failure she wanted to forget. Though George was unmarried, she knew he was not the marrying type. He was up front about not wanting a wife and children. Shelley thought she could change his mind, but the only thing he changed was his partner. He began dating a voluptuous brunette named Sophie, who worked as a waitress.

One night, while they were out to dinner, Shelley noticed that the waitress acted as if she knew George. As she took their order, she smiled at him in a way that spoke volumes. When Shelley asked George if he knew her, he cleared his throat and mentioned that he had eaten there before. Shelley was certain that the waitress was one of George's side dishes. Their relationship ended abruptly the next day.

Picking up the phone, she buzzed the receptionist.

"Lynn, I have some urgent personal business to take care of. Please cancel all my appointments for the day."

Before Lynn could inquire about the reason for her sudden departure, Shelley continued, "I have to leave immediately."

Shelley rose and grabbed her black Gucci purse from her desk drawer then walked to the closet and reached for her black leather coat. She shivered as she wrapped the coat around her and tied the belt. Looking into the mirror, she wiped off the black mascara that was smudged beneath her hazel eyes. Putting on her gloves, she left her office and ignored Lynn, who made an attempt to speak to her.

"I'll be in touch with you later," Shelley said as she breezed by Lynn's desk on her way out of the office.

In the parking garage, she headed for her silver Ford Mustang with determination. Fumbling for her keys, she started the car. The screeching of the wheels as she exited the garage even startled her. She definitely felt out of control.

Shelley glanced in the rear-view mirror. For a split second, she thought she saw someone sitting on the back seat.

"Must have been a shadow," she reasoned. As she stopped for a red light, she pulled out a cigarette and lit it. She was going to stop smoking, but it didn't matter anymore.

Again, she thought she saw something move in the back seat. Shifting her body around, she could see that no one was in her car. She turned up the heater, feeling that same chill in the air she had experienced in her office.

The last time she felt that coldness around her was when she met Mark at a restaurant in Indianapolis.

Shelley recalled that they went to a Steak and Ale and sat in a booth far removed from the other tables. It was a cool October evening. Mark had separated from his wife and was living in a studio apartment in downtown Indianapolis. They began seeing each other three or four times a week.

The waitress delivered the menus and they ordered drinks. She requested a Stinger and he chose a bourbon on the rocks. She was relieved that the waitress was a middle-aged woman. Shelley had commented to Mark that the drink would warm her up. He insisted that the room was comfortable, though he had been cold earlier that day.

"Why this memory, now?" thought Shelley.

Then she recalled that when she returned to her car, and as she drove back to her apartment, she had glanced at the back seat several times, thinking someone was behind her, and remembered that she was so cold then, too. Shaking her head, she glanced one more time in her rear-view mirror.

"Just as I thought. It's all in my imagination."

CHAPTER 6
NICK TROIANO

"Repent, for the kingdom of heaven is at hand."
(Matthew 3:2)

Nick Troiano picked up the phone in his well-furnished office on the thirteenth floor of the fairly new downtown Brooklyn office building. His desk had numerous folders on it. Contracts ready for his signature were piled before him. T-Men Inc. was Nick's construction business. He and his brothers, Tom and Charlie, had a lucrative business that served the five boroughs of New York.

"Mr. Troiano, the deal we spoke about is sealed. Any further instructions?"

Nick smiled and glanced at his watch.

"No, Frank."

At noon, Frank had taken care of a nuisance, swiftly and permanently.

Turning to his lawyer, Lawrence Klein, Nick motioned that their meeting was ended.

"Larry, let's have lunch. I have a terrific appetite today."

Nick was a little under six feet tall. In his early forties, his salt and pepper hair was always perfectly styled. His dark brown eyes had an intense look to them. His expensive taste in clothing was obvious. He wore only the best in custom-made suits. His casual clothing usually consisted of jogging suits and running shoes, though nothing he did approximated an athletic activity in his free time. He had promised his wife he would work out, lose twenty-five pounds and stop smoking Cuban cigars. Whenever she reminded him of his promise, he would simply tell her he was working on it.

They stood up and walked out of the office. Turning to his secretary, Nick indicated that he would return around two o'clock.

"Mr. Troiano, your wife called a few minutes ago. She wants to know if you are going to be home this evening in time for your son's play at school."

"Call Lisa back and tell her I'll meet her at the school. I have some important business to take care of late this afternoon."

Nick and Larry exited the building. A black stretch limousine stopped in front of the building. The chauffeur opened the back door for Nick, who slid clumsily into the back seat. Larry was in tow.

"Have a drink with me, Larry," Nick said as he poured himself a glass of whiskey. Larry obediently took his drink.

Nick Troiano was notorious in New York City for his involvement in the Mafia, but there was never enough proof to indict him for criminal activities. However, both his brothers had been in and out of prison. The curious thing was that people who crossed Nick disappeared mysteriously or refused to make statements against him, citing memory loss as the motive.

Nick prided himself on being a family man. Only his three children looked up to him with unconditional love and devotion. Nick may have been a complicated man with many facets to his personality, but to his children he was only one thing, their daddy who loved and cared for them.

While Nick was courting Lisa, she was definitely impressed with his family's wealth. However, when she discovered that Nick was a member of a crime family, her mind did battle with her heart. By the time she found out about his family's "business," she had fallen deeply in love with him. Though not a Pollyanna type, Lisa did hold out hope that the goodness she discovered in Nick would eventually prevail over the influences of his family.

In fact, he promised her that he would find ways to build up the legitimate businesses of the Troiano brothers so they could quit their illegal activities. She wasn't sure anymore if she believed him at the time or wanted to believe him.

Nick's family originally came from Palermo, Sicily, in the early part of the last century. Their father, Nicolo, began the family's introduction into the Mafia, American-style. Though not an educated man, Nicolo had a keen intellect and the ability to organize and recruit others to conduct profitable, but illegal activities. Carefully considering the vices of men, he launched illegal enterprises that included gambling, bootlegging, embezzlement and loan-sharking.

Shortly after college, Nick and his brothers began a more profound descent into the family business. By the time he met his wife, the former Lisa Thomas, he was already knee-deep in deception and lawlessness while at the same time trying to build up T-Men Inc.

While visiting an uncle recovering from heart bypass surgery at Methodist Hospital in the Bronx, Nick met Lisa, a social worker on the staff. Later, he told her that he instantly fell in love with her and knew she was the woman for him.

Lisa was no beauty, and she knew it. She would often make light of her looks by telling people that Nick fell in love with her compassionate side. When she would look at herself in the mirror, her eyes immediately focused on her thin brown hair that was extremely hard to style or shape. She hated her protruding ears. She was, however, grateful for her model's figure. She often wished for a face to match her body.

Lisa was always loyal to Nick. Several years into the marriage, she questioned Nick about his promise to build up T-Men Inc. and his plan to legitimize his businesses. He would simply tell her that he was working on it.

They had been married for ten years before Lisa seriously considered separating from him after overhearing a conversation between her husband and Larry.

"Nick, what if the police question you about Mitch's accident? You are neighbors."

"I'll just tell them I have no knowledge of the accident. Surely they won't think I had anything to do with it. After all, my wife, Lisa, and his wife, Judy, are the best of friends."

Lisa stood frozen in the hallway as she realized that Nick had ordered Mitch killed. A week earlier, Nicky Jr. had been hospitalized for a concussion and broken ribs after Mitch had accidentally hit him as he was backing his car out of his driveway. Nicky was not permitted to use his skateboard in the street since he was only 6 years old. But that day, he ventured out into the street and was in the wrong place at the wrong time.

Mitch immediately called for an ambulance and did all he could to help Nicky. At the hospital, he cried like a baby.

"I didn't see him! One second the street was clear, and the next minute there was your son."

Lisa understood it was a terrible accident, but Nick was livid. Though he reassured Mitch that he held nothing against him, Lisa knew that Nick blamed Mitch for his son's injuries. Now, overhearing the conversation between Nick and Larry confirmed in Lisa's mind that she was married to a vicious killer, and she wanted out.

Lisa learned through the years that Nick could never be crossed. How could she liberate herself from this beast she had married? She could never ask for a separation or divorce. No one walked out on Nick Troiano. She needed a different approach. She decided to tell him she wanted to relocate to Florida part of the year. After all, her parents and her sisters lived there.

She would explain to Nick that her aging parents needed her. Her father's recent bout with cancer helped bring her to this decision. Since Lisa and Nick had no financial concerns, she and the children could return frequently to Brooklyn to visit Nick, and he could fly down to see them whenever he wanted.

Nick stared at her with those intense dark brown eyes as she spoke. Without warning, he grabbed her by both shoulders. Slowly, he released his grip and told her in no uncertain terms that she and the children would remain in Brooklyn. It was as though he read her thoughts and figured out her strategy to get away from him.

Taking her face between his hands, he kissed his wife on the lips. He gently adjusted her thin, limp brown hair and looked into her soft brown eyes.

"You're staying right here. You want to visit your folks for a week, go ahead. You go without the kids and you return in a week."

Lisa understood that there was no way out of her marriage.

Months after Mitch's burial, Lisa learned from Judy that Nick had set up an extremely generous trust fund for their children. Lisa was surprised that Judy never suspected Nick's role in her husband's unfortunate accident on the subway tracks. A homeless man was seen pushing Mitch to his death. But the police never found the homeless man, who seemed to disappear into thin air.

In the limo, Nick turned to Larry.

"You know, Larry, life is very fragile. Look at 9/11 and what happened at the Twin Towers. You know Peters, that district attorney who has been rattling my cage? You need to tell him that life is very fragile. You never know when a terrorist can strike! He needs to get his priorities straight."

Nick laughed heartily.

Larry shook his head in agreement.

"Understood, Nick."

Turning to Larry, Nick commented on how cold he felt. Larry agreed. He instructed the chauffeur to turn the heat up.

CHAPTER 7
MICHAEL REID

"What do you think? If a man has a hundred sheep, and one of them has gone astray, does he not leave the ninety-nine on the mountains and go in search of the one that went astray? And if he finds it, truly, I say to you, he rejoices over it more than over the ninety-nine that never went astray. So it is not the will of my Father who is in heaven that one of these little ones should perish."
(Matthew 18:12–14)

Michael Reid, professor of sociology at Brooklyn College, walked from Boylan Hall with books under his arm and a briefcase in his hand. He was on his way to James Hall to prepare for an interview for his new book entitled *Religion and Death in American Society*.

Michael was tall and thin with thick black hair and light gray eyes. He was strikingly handsome. He was as vain as he was attractive. Like many of the other professors in his department, Michael dressed very informally, usually in jeans and casual shirts. He wanted to blend in with his students.

He often traveled to class from his apartment in Flatlands by riding his ten-speed bicycle. At 29 years old, he easily could have passed for ten years younger. With some careful evaluation, his emotional age could be placed somewhere between 18 to 21 years old.

"Hey, Professor Reid."

He turned around to see a young woman, a freshman, who had a crush on him. She was a student in his Sociology of Religion class.

"Today, you said that you don't believe in God."

"Hello. Rebecca, isn't it?"

"My friends call me Becky."

"That's correct. I am an atheist."

"You weren't always an atheist, right?"

"I was raised as a Catholic, in fact. After high school, I began to re-evaluate my beliefs. I concluded that God did not exist. No reasonable person can believe in God. Will you excuse me, Rebecca? I'm in a rush. I need to prepare for an important interview. Maybe we can talk another time over lunch."

"But Professor Reid, if God doesn't exist then what's the point in trying to improve society? Why try to understand society? It's all going to end anyway! Life has no real meaning!"

"Rebecca, I really must go. Life does have meaning, the meaning you give it."

As he smiled at his student, he could see that she was visibly upset.

"That's always how it is when you begin to doubt your faith," Michael thought as he crossed the campus to James Hall.

He was less concerned with the meaning of existence at the moment or his student's crisis of faith, and more focused on his immediate need to get warm. He had been extremely cold all morning despite his layered clothing.

"I must be coming down with something."

Michael always enjoyed telling his students he was an atheist. For some strange reason, it made him feel superior.

"God is for wimps," he would often tell himself.

If the truth be told, Michael liked to single himself out as a free and independent thinker who had no need of God, organized religion or organized government. For someone with a doctorate in sociology, he often failed to bring his opinions to their ultimate conclusions. What was more unfortunate was that his life lacked depth and purpose.

As he entered James Hall, he stopped to chat with another professor from his department. Professor Trudy Himmelfarb was in her late forties and had been teaching at the college for ten years.

"So, I hear you're leaving Brooklyn College."

Trudy looked at her colleague with sadness in her eyes.

"Michael, Vick and I are divorcing after fifteen years of marriage. I need a change. The kids need a change. We're moving back to Rhode Island to be close to my side of the family."

"I'm sorry for your situation. But statistics do show that almost half of all marriages end in divorce. You and Vick lasted longer than most. I'll never marry. I prefer the safety of non-permanent serial relationships. The archaic and barbaric straight-jacket known as matrimony should be illegal."

Trudy knew she could always count on Michael to be an insensitive jerk.

Taking a deep breath, she responded, "Well, I'd love to stand and chat with you, but I need to get ready for my next lecture. Good seeing you."

As she turned to walk away from him, she shook her head.

"If he ever married, he would become a statistic. His wife would end up killing him!"

Michael watched as Trudy walked away from him. The sad look in her eyes reminded him of the look in his mother's eyes the day she announced that she and his father were divorcing. For Michael, that was the worst day in his life. His world was destroyed by five words: "We are getting a divorce."

He remembered being very angry with his father that weekend. He watched as his father loaded a small U-Haul truck that he hooked to his car. His mother and his sister, Kathleen, went to his maternal grandmother's house. Michael insisted on remaining home for his father's grand exit.

"Well, son, I'm glad you stayed behind. Why don't you give me a hand with some of these boxes?"

Michael proceeded to help his father pack the U-Haul.

"This is what death must feel like," he thought.

When they finished putting all his father's belongings in the truck, he and his father, who by this time had worked up a sweat, rummaged in the refrigerator for something cold to drink. They sat down at the kitchen table.

"Why, Dad?"

Michael's father looked at his son.

"I'll always love your mother, but I don't love her as a wife anymore. The marriage has been over for some time now. I don't expect you to understand."

Then he proceeded to tell his son that they had married young, shortly after college. What began as an adventure became a boring routine.

"Our marriage was like soda pop without the fizz."

At the time, Michael found that analogy startling. His father tried to assure Michael that he still loved his mother, but he needed to begin a new life.

"Son, I've forgotten who I am. I need to rediscover myself and live again."

"But, Mom still loves you. You still have love for her. Couldn't you try to find yourself again with her, and with us?"

"It should be that easy!"

Michael couldn't understand what his father was searching for in life. Even less comprehensible was his father's need to break up their family. He simply wanted his parents to be back together. As the weeks passed, Michael thought about marriage. If love couldn't cement a marriage together, what could?

CHAPTER 8
JAY ROKER

O Lord, thou hast searched me and known me! Thou knowest when I sit down and when I rise up; thou discernest my thoughts from afar. Thou searchest out my path and my lying down, and art acquainted with all my ways.
(Psalm 139:1–3)

Saturday, December 8

Jay Roker parked his Eagle Jeep along the busy avenue in Queens. When he had returned from the convenience store in Jackson Heights the previous day, he tried to start the car one more time. It started with no problem. Even the "check engine" warning light had gone out.

"My luck may be changing."

Jay was the first person to arrive at the Caring Clinic for Women.

As a security guard, Jay's job was to keep those anti-abortion people in line. It was his role to provide women with full access to reproductive services. He had often mused that he was not totally sold on abortion, but the job paid his rent, although barely.

"My job is a necessary evil," he would tell friends and family members.

Barely 25 years old, he hoped that his luck would change in the near future and he would be able to move on to a more comfortable job.

Jay stood outside. He was bundled up but was still shivering.

"Maybe I could audition as a double for Denzel Washington," he mused.

As his nose began to run from the cold, he spotted Pat Marino making her way to the clinic. She always looked like she had just stepped out of a fashion magazine. With streaked brown hair falling beneath her shoulders and her long red wool coat with a black velvet collar and black suede heeled boots, Pat could have been a model on the cover of *Vogue*. He politely opened the door for her.

Pat glared at the sidewalk counselors and the prayer group, and gave Jay her usual one-liner, "They should get a life."

Though no one else knew, Pat resented the presence of the sidewalk counselors because they caused her to remember her own abortion for a split second, and her initial desire to have Paul's baby. Why, then, did she choose to work in an abortion clinic, if she wanted to forget? She wasn't sure.

To her own surprise, she became a committed supporter of a woman's right to choose. When the Caring Clinic for Women was looking for a new receptionist, she interviewed for the job and was pleased to be hired.

When her parents found out about her new job, all hell broke loose in the Marino house. Pat held her ground despite the ongoing lectures about right and wrong that she would hear from her parents on a regular basis. Once, they confronted their daughter and asked her whether she had an abortion.

Her response was total denial. Her parents knew instinctively that she was lying. They resolved not to push her over the edge, and too far away from them to ever reach her.

Jay smiled as Pat entered the clinic. But then he looked at those people praying and felt a tinge of guilt. He remembered his own sister's decision not to have an abortion three years ago. He had been the one who drove her to a clinic in Manhattan. But after talking to some sidewalk counselors, she decided to have her baby.

At first, Jay questioned the wisdom of her decision. But now, three years later, little Duane was definitely the best thing that ever happened to the family.

"This kid can light up your day with his smile," he thought.

Sadly, he opened the door for a beautiful African-American girl, who was obviously struggling with her decision. He could see her swollen eyes and the sad look on her face. She smiled back at the sidewalk counselors.

Being an African-American, Jay noted that the majority of the women who came to the Caring Clinic for Women were also African-Americans. That bothered him.

"Tanisha, we'll help you. You don't have to do this. You and your baby deserve better than this," said one of the middle-aged women, who was very kind to Jay. Recently, she had given him a basket of child's toys that she had won at a fundraiser. Duane was delighted.

"I hope that girl listens to those folks," thought Jay.

CHAPTER 9
PAT MARINO

Even before a word is on my tongue, lo, O Lord, thou knowest it altogether. Thou dost beset me behind and before, and layest thy hand upon me.

(Psalm 139:4–5)

Pat Marino sat at the reception desk and started to look over the schedule of appointments. The names all appeared so strangely familiar to her. She glanced at the wall clock that read seven-fifteen. Jay admitted the first five morning appointments.

Keshia Boyd, a 20-year-old African-American woman, placed her money on Pat's desk. She was visibly nervous.

"I've never had an abortion before. I'm not sure I'm doing the right thing."

"Relax. Everything will be O.K. It's a routine procedure. Before you know it, it will be all over. You'll feel much better."

"Are you sure?"

"It's always a difficult choice. No one comes in here delighted to have an abortion. It's something you have to do. Here is your receipt. Sign here and here."

Denise and Brenda were already seated in the waiting room. Another girl stood at the windows and watched as the sidewalk counselors approached people entering the clinic. She turned to Denise, who was closest to her.

"Who are those people outside with those signs?"

Denise knew exactly who they were. They were sidewalk counselors. In one of her law classes, the whole concept of the constitutional right to free speech was discussed.

"They oppose abortion and want to offer women other options," Denise stated flatly.

"Don't they realize how hard this is for us? They should mind their own business. What other options do we have, anyway? All we can do is keep the baby or put it up for adoption."

Another girl added sarcastically, "I ain't gonna give up my baby after carrying it for nine months. No way."

For some reason, this last statement really unnerved Denise.

"They believe your pregnancy is their business," said a woman in scrubs. "We've been trying to get rid of them for years. See that line by the door? If they cross it, we'll have them arrested. It's private property."

Denise recalled her law professor's comments regarding First Amendment rights. One of the students suggested that sidewalk counseling was a form of harassment.

"Those people should be arrested. It's not their business to be out there telling people what choices to make."

The law professor listened attentively to the female law student, who was radically pro-choice.

"If we were to accept the pro-choice argument regarding the First Amendment, only abortionists and those in the abortion industry would have the right to express their opinions. Does that sound like a democracy to you? Silencing those who are pro-life would be setting a very dangerous precedent. Sidewalk counselors present viable options for women confronted by problem pregnancies. Why would you consider their presence a form of harassment?"

The woman in scrubs shut the blinds at the bay window, shielding the women from the prayer group. She called out the name of the first woman scheduled for an abortion, but there was no response.

"Tanisha?"

One of the other girls indicated that Tanisha had gone back outside to speak to the sidewalk counselors.

The woman in the blue scrubs looked annoyed as her mouth formed a straight line. She peered carefully through the blinds to see if Tanisha was being harassed. She noticed that Tanisha had accepted a rosary as one of the counselors smiled and spoke to her.

Snapping the blinds back into place, she turned to a beautiful Mexican girl, whose Indian features were striking. She spoke little English. Her jet-black hair was straight and hung down to her waist. Her complexion was on the light side of brown and her eyes were almost black. She appeared to be under 18 years of age.

"Claudia, you're next. Do you speak English?"

"Juan, her boyfriend, responded, "She speaks English, but you need to speak slowly."

The timid Hispanic girl rose from her seat. She glanced at her *novio,* Juan, who kissed her affectionately. Uttering something in Spanish, he began to make his exit from the clinic, but only after he was sure that Claudia had been escorted downstairs.

CHAPTER 10
DR. SAMUEL WEISS

Whither shall I go from thy Spirit? Or whither shall I flee from thy presence? If I ascend to heaven, thou art there! If I make my bed in Sheol, thou art there!

(Psalm 139:7–8)

Sam Weiss slid out of his leather-covered car seat and walked quickly to the side entrance of the Caring Clinic for Women. The last thing he wanted was to dialogue with those fanatics. What especially drove him crazy was that some of them were very pleasant to him and assured him that they would pray for him and his family.

"They need to get a life."

Just as he was about to step on the curb, one of the "fanatics" called out to him, "You left your car door open."

With an air of impatience, Sam called out, "Thanks."

"We're praying for you. You know, you delivered my daughter twenty-five years ago at Victory Memorial Hospital. You were a good obstetrician. Why this?"

For a split second, Sam wanted to engage the man in conversation. His own daughter, Helene, would have been 35 years old. The deep wound of his daughter's tragic death would never heal. She was only 11 years old when a drunk driver hit her while she was walking home from school. She was in a coma for three weeks then everything that could go wrong did go wrong. Ethel was devastated beyond words.

"Why did I become an abortionist? Why did I buy this facility? Why not? The girls would do it anyway. The money was very good. Some of these babies didn't have a chance at happiness anyway. He was doing these girls a favor," Sam thought to himself.

In his own defense, Sam yelled back, "They have a right to choose!" Even to his ears, this excuse sounded lame.

As Sam slipped into the building, he heard the man reply, "Only God can choose life or death."

Sam remembered the day he learned that his precious daughter, Helene, had died.

This time, he yelled back at the man, "No, no. We choose life and death. God has nothing to do with it."

Breathing heavily, he walked into his clinic to begin his day.

"In a few more years, I'll have enough money to retire and enjoy life," he thought.

Sam walked into his office and sat at his desk. He loosened his tie and gazed at the framed photograph of his wife and daughter on his desk.

"I wonder who it was that I delivered twenty-five years ago?"

He picked up the picture and examined Helene's face. He tried to imagine what she would look like today at age 35. He wondered who she would have married and how many children she would have had.

"That drunken creep robbed us of a lifetime of memories," Sam thought. "He should rot in hell."

CHAPTER 11
DENISE SMITH
AND BRENDA HERMANN

For thou didst form my inward parts, thou didst knit me together in my mother's womb. I praise thee, for thou art fearful and wonderful. Wonderful are thy works! Thou knowest me right well; my frame was not hidden from thee, when I was being made in secret, intricately wrought in the depths of the earth.

(Psalm 139:13–15)

Denise and Brenda sat side by side in the clinic waiting room.

"Don't worry, Denise. I've known plenty of women who have had abortions. You won't feel a thing."

"Brenda, do you think I'm making the right choice?"

"What else can you do? Greg doesn't want the baby and you both need to finish law school. Think, girl. This is not the time to be knitting baby booties!"

"I know, but something inside of me just tells me not to do it. My mother and father would have a fit if they knew!"

"Your mother had five kids, for God's sake. And didn't she have a miscarriage or two? Anyway, that was her choice to have five children. That doesn't mean you have to do what she did, right?"

"Brenda, I don't know about this. It seems wrong to me, very wrong."

"Denise, get a hold of yourself. Remember when I thought I was pregnant last year? What did you say to me?"

"I told you that I would support whatever decision you made. But you turned out not to be pregnant!"

"Denise, this was an accident. You yourself told me that. Think of how your life will change with a baby! You're feeling guilty because of your family's values. But you have to live your own life and decide what is right and wrong for you."

"What is right and wrong? Can it be right for me and wrong for my mother?" wondered Denise.

Tired of talking, Denise sat back and closed her eyes.

"Can it be wrong for one person and right for another? Is morality a subjective thing? Is God's law the same or different for people?"

Her mind drifted back to her days as an undergraduate student at St. Vincent's University. Monsignor Joseph Noone, one of her favorite professors, taught the Moral Theology class. Some unpopular topics, such as artificial contraception, premarital sex, homosexuality, abortion and euthanasia, were discussed. Monsignor presented the teachings of the Catholic Church. A non-Christian student challenged the notion that the Catholic Church taught the truth about morality.

"Monsignor, as a non-Christian, I have to tell you that what's true for you is not true for me. I don't believe in the Church's tenets or its position on most of the issues you've presented. I do believe that all religions are essentially equal since we all have the same God."

Monsignor Noone thanked the young man for contributing his opinion.

"Most religions attempt to understand God or to explain the relationship between humanity and a supreme being or beings. However, many of these belief systems contradict each other or contradict Christianity. They cannot all be true at the same time."

"O.K., but all these religions may have some truth."

"But that's not what you just said. You said that all religions were equal. Jason, would you say that there's a connection between truth and reality?"

"Certainly, there's a connection," responded Jason.

Taking a large book in his hands, Monsignor Noone dropped it abruptly to the floor. The sound of the book hitting the floor drew the attention of the students.

"I am either holding the book in my hands or it is on the floor at this very moment. Correct?"

Jason shook his head in agreement.

Placing a pen in his open hand, Monsignor Noone continued, "This is either a pen or a bird in my hand. Which is it, Jason?"

"A pen, of course."

"The truth must be based on reality."

Monsignor Noone lifted the book from the floor, opened it and began quoting from it.

"'The fundamental and self-evident rule of being and logic refutes religious pluralism.' Would anyone like to apply this statement to our present discussion and how this relates to reality and truth?"

Denise volunteered.

"Well, Christianity and its beliefs cannot be true and false at the same time. All religions cannot be true in their entirety if they contradict or are in opposition to what Christianity teaches."

"Why can't they all be true?"

"Because Christianity is based on Divine Revelation. The God of the Christians is real and what he reveals is truth. It would be absurd to conclude that the God of truth would lie about himself by offering contradictory revelations about himself."

Before Denise could recall the rest of the dialogue in class, the woman in the blue scrubs reappeared.

"Denise, it's time to go downstairs. They are ready for you."

"Oh, Brenda!"

"May I go with her downstairs?"

"Sorry, only the patient goes downstairs."

Denise slowly rose from her seat, leaving all her personal items of value with Brenda. Embracing each other, they parted.

Pat walked slowly to the elevator and suddenly felt so cold that she trembled.

Taking the elevator down one flight, Denise found herself standing in a very long hallway. Another attendant greeted her and led her to the area where she changed into a hospital gown. As she undressed, the last thing she removed was her crucifix. She pinned up her long blonde hair and stared at the crucifix she had received on her Confirmation when she was in the seventh grade. She wanted to turn and run.

Denise had taken the name Maria, for St. Maria Goretti, as her Confirmation name. She had heard the story of this young martyr's life and was impressed with her desire to preserve her purity, even if it meant death.

"I was so young and so innocent back then," thought Denise.

Sister Regina, her religion teacher at the time, tried to impress on her students their need to consider their bodies "temples of the Holy Spirit."

"What would Sister Regina think of me now!" she thought.

Again, Denise's mind wandered back to her undergraduate school days. She remembered Dr. Michael Sullivan's Theology class and his exposition on faith and reason.

"What moves us to believe is not the fact that revealed truths appear as true and intelligible in the light or our natural reason. We believe 'because of the authority of God himself, who reveals them, who can neither deceive nor be deceived.' "

Denise knew the Church's teaching on abortion, yet as the nurse inquired about which arm she wanted the I.V. inserted in, she responded, "This one."

Denise lifted her left arm. The I.V. was hooked up after several attempts to find the vein.

"It's too late to turn back now," she thought.

The nurse told Denise to relax. The doctor would be in shortly. Looking up at the nurse, Denise indicated that she was ambivalent about the procedure. The nurse simply reassured her that it would be over quickly and she would feel a lot better.

Those were the last words Denise remembered hearing before the procedure.

Part II—The Awakening

CHAPTER 12
DENISE SMITH

"Life is only for Love; Time is only to find God."
(St. Bernard)

And he told them a parable, saying, "The land of a rich man brought forth plentifully; and he thought to himself, 'What shall I do, for I have nowhere to store my crops?' And he said, 'I will do this: I will pull down my barns, and build larger ones; and there I will store all my grain and my goods. And I will say to my soul, Soul, you have ample goods laid up for many years; take your ease, eat, drink, be merry.' But God said to him, 'Fool! This night your soul is required of you; and the things you have prepared, whose will they be?' So is he who lays up treasure for himself, and is not rich toward God."
(Luke 12:16–21)

Denise awoke on a gurney with yellow curtains drawn around her. She felt drowsy and had no pain. She was covered with a thin sheet, but felt terribly cold. Relieved that the procedure was over, she wanted only to get out of the clinic and back to her ordinary life in Brooklyn.

According to their plan, Brenda would pick up Denise and bring her to her home in Oyster Bay, Long Island. Denise would stay in Brenda's basement apartment for a couple of days. Though Brenda's basement apartment was in the Hermann home, there would be little or no contact with her parents.

As Denise thought about the next seventy-two hours, her mind focused on her relationship with Greg and their dialogue about her abortion.

"Denise, we have goals. We both want to become lawyers. A child just doesn't fit into the scheme of things."

"Greg, I honestly don't want to have a baby right now, but the thought of an abortion frightens me."

"Well, no couple anticipates having an unplanned pregnancy, right? No couple is overjoyed to abort a pregnancy! What else can we do?"

Denise and Greg were not ready to commit to marriage or to a family. She had no other option but to abort the pregnancy. Or was there another option?

For whatever reason, a memory kept surfacing as she glanced at the plastic bracelet the nurse had put on her wrist. The memory was of Denise's mother after she lost her baby. She recalled her mother sitting in the den with a cigar box on her lap.

Her mother was looking into the box and crying.

"Mommy, why are you crying?"

Maggie turned to Denise, wiped the tears from her eyes and smiled.

"Come here, you little munchkin."

She opened her arms to pick up Denise.

"Honey, I'm crying because I lost your little brother. God took him to heaven. It hurts, but I know that it was God's will for Joshua."

"Why did God take Joshua? Didn't he know that we wanted him?"

"Oh, yes, God knew we wanted Joshua. That's a hard question to answer. What I can tell you is that Joshua is happy because he is in our heavenly Father's loving arms. We'll see Joshua someday when it's time to go to heaven."

Denise wasn't sure she understood all that, but was pleased that her mother stopped crying.

"So, what's in the cigar box?"

Maggie lifted her plastic hospital bracelet to show it to Denise.

"This is all I have to remember Joshua. I wore it while he was still with me. I'll keep it in this box to remember him."

Denise looked into the cigar box.

"You have a lot of junk in that box."

Maggie laughed.

"No, Denise, I have a lot of memories in this box."

Picking up a piece of plastic no bigger than two square inches, she showed her daughter a blonde curl.

"This is a lock of your hair when you were a year old. See your name and date on the tag?"

"Mommy, I'm gonna find you a bigger box for your memories. I think you're gonna need one."

Maggie closed the box and put it aside. She kissed her daughter.

"Why don't we go into the kitchen and see if we can find some of those chocolate chip cookies I baked the other day?"

Denise stared at the plastic bracelet around her own wrist. Denise did not have a miscarriage and she was not in a hospital. She covered her face with both hands.

"I don't need any memories!"

Taking her hands away from her face, she raised herself on her elbows.

"Nurse, may I have a blanket? I'm extremely cold."

There was no answer. Denise waited for a response. She repeated her request several times with no response. Sliding her legs over the side of the gurney, she reached for the curtains and parted them. There were three other cubicles with curtains. She dared not pull them aside.

"Nurse, can I have a blanket? I'm freezing!"

Again, she waited for a response.

"Nurse. Doctor. Someone please help me!"

No one responded.

Denise stood up. The tiled floor was very cold. She walked toward the door and gently turned the knob and looked down the hallway. She saw no one. She glanced at the wall clock. It read eight-fifteen in the morning.

Cautiously, Denise walked back to each of the three curtained off areas in the room. Calling out to find out if someone lay behind the curtain, she gently moved each curtain aside. Each gurney was empty. Returning to the door leading to the hallway, she opened it and slipped into the hallway. Before doing so, she wrapped a sheet around herself.

"What is going on here?"

Denise walked out into the hallway. She called out for help as she shivered under the thin sheet. She made her way to the next room and knocked on the door. There was no answer. There was total silence, an eerie silence, an unnatural silence.

She began walking quickly up and down the hallway. Opening one door after the other, she saw no one. She saw what appeared to be suction machines, oxygen tanks and other colored tanks, gurneys and instruments on trays lined with white linens.

Panic seized Denise as she looked up at the hallway clock. It showed that it was still eight-fifteen, but at least fifteen minutes had passed since she awoke. She noticed that the hands of the clock didn't move. The hand that should have shown the passing seconds was frozen in place.

Denise raced back to the elevator and pressed the call button. She entered and pressed the button for the first floor. As she exited and walked a few feet, she could see that both the receptionist's desk and the waiting room were empty. The lights were dimmed.

"What on earth is going on?"

Denise ran to the front doors of the Caring Clinic for Women and tried to open them. They didn't budge. She ran to the reception area and called out for Brenda. She ran over to the large bay window and pulled up the thin slatted blinds. Not one car passed by and not one person could be seen on the streets.

"Where are those sidewalk counselors? Oh, God, what's happening?"

Denise ran back to the front door and desperately tried to open it again. Then she ran back to the window. She pounded on the window with both fists until they stung.

Remembering that there was a side door to the clinic, Denise raced to it. It had a panic bar and should open easily. As she depressed the bar, the door remained locked. She slid to the floor in tears.

"Oh, God, please help me!"

Suddenly, out of the corner of her eye, she saw a man approaching her. Denise stood up. The man was tall and handsome, perhaps in his thirties, dressed too elegantly to be a doctor or employee of the clinic. Denise felt an overwhelming sense of dread as she faced him.

CHAPTER 13
PAT MARINO

Then I said, "Lo, I come; in the roll of the book it is written of me; I delight to do thy will, O my God; thy law is within my heart."

(Psalm 40:7–8)

Pat rummaged through her bag looking for her pocket calendar. She wasn't sure if she was supposed to meet her parents for dinner that evening or the following evening. She noticed that their dinner was scheduled for the following Saturday evening.

"That's a relief," she thought.

Pat was grateful for long lapses of time between visits. She had to gather her strength to deal with the Marino duo.

In recent years, Dom and Louise made a point of keeping the lines of communication open with Pat. As a child, Pat was very stubborn and unresponsive to her parents' orders when she felt they were trying to control her. Often, she would be punished just for giving them that look of disdain for their authority.

"The look" was Pat's way of saying, "Leave me the hell alone."

"We tell you things for your own good, Pat. Someday you will be a parent and understand."

Pat never understood and never believed that she would understand. What she did understand was that growing up in the Marino household meant having to conform. She and her brother, Joe, and her sister, Carrie, towed the line, at least outwardly.

No child of Dom and Louise Marino was going to stay out until all hours of the night. No child of Dom and Louise Marino was going to cut out of school. No child of Dom and Louise Marino was going to miss Mass on Sundays. The list went on and on.

Pat was convinced that her parents were placed on Earth to make her life miserable. She chaffed under their authority and challenged it at every possible opportunity. When she landed her first job after college, she was delighted because she had discovered her ticket to independence. She was no longer going to do as her parents dictated. In fact, she was going to do as she damn well pleased. Moving out was the first order of business.

The week Pat moved out, Carrie, her younger sister, a freshman at New York University, sat on her bed as she packed her last possessions.

"I wish I were moving out with you," Carrie said with a note of sadness in her voice.

"Well, you can visit, but not too often."

"Gee, thanks a lot!"

Pat loved her sister, but she loved her freedom a lot more. Carrie did not have the same problems with her parents that she did. Carrie conformed to the Marino code of law. Her older brother, Joe, who was already out on his own, knew how to manage his parents while he lived under their authoritarian roof.

She once told him, "Joe, you need to go into politics. If you worked the crowds like you work Mom and Dad, you would be elected President of the United States!"

He simply smiled.

"Your problem, Pat, is that you have a big mouth. You're always trying to tell Mom and Dad what you are not going to do. Did you ever try to please them by doing what they asked of you? This would be a novel approach! Anyway, they don't hassle me because I don't make a federal issue out of everything like you do."

Maybe he was right. But just maybe she was right most of the time!

Pat looked down at her wristwatch. It was almost noon.

"O.K., time for lunch."

Today, she'd order Chinese. Since she had recovered from her flu-like symptoms the other day, her appetite had returned to normal. She picked up her phone to dial the take-out restaurant two blocks away, but there was no dial tone.

"Great, now we have a problem with the phones!"

Pat moved away from the reception desk and walked past the waiting room.

"Hey, where are all the patients?"

She walked to the front door to see if they had gone outside to talk to the "fanatics" or just smoke cigarettes. They weren't allowed to smoke in the waiting area. It was an unhealthy habit. She attempted to turn the doorknob and take a look outside, but the knob wouldn't turn. She knocked on the door and called out Jay's name.

"Open the door from the outside, Jay. It's stuck."

Pat heard no reply.

"Great!"

She began to walk down the hallway to the room where the accountant was working on the books.

"Bob, you won't believe this, but I can't open the front door."

As she said this, she realized that Bob was not in the office. Turning around, Pat decided to go downstairs.

"Surely everyone has not gone to lunch!"

Pat could feel her heart pounding furiously within her chest.

The elevator doors opened, and Pat entered and pressed the button for the basement. The door shut, but the elevator didn't move. The light in the elevator dimmed until she stood in complete darkness.

Feeling for the buttons, she pressed the large protruding red button that sounded an alarm. She was stuck on a darkened elevator with no way out. After several minutes, the alarm discontinued its shrill sound. Pat felt trapped. Who would hear her screams? Where was everyone? What was happening? Why was it so cold?

Suddenly, the light came back on and the elevator began its descent. Reaching the basement, the doors parted. Pat immediately stepped into the hallway.

Shaking, she proceeded down the hall, calling out the names of the other employees.

"Cindy, Cathy, anybody here?"

No one responded. Carefully, she entered room after room, skipping the rooms at the further end where the abortions were performed. All the rooms were empty. Then she heard one of the suction machines being used. As she slowly approached the room where she heard the sound come from, the door opened by itself. Afraid to look in the room, but drawn to it, she peered inside. The suction machine was silent again. The room was empty.

Trembling with fear, she ran to the back door and tried to depress the panic bar in order to escape. It wouldn't budge.

"What on earth?"

She turned and ran to the elevator then decided that she wasn't going to take that elevator again. She approached the door to the stairway, but like the other doors it was locked. She had no choice but to try the elevator. Shaking violently and shivering from the cold, she entered the elevator and pressed the button for the first floor, hoping that it would function. The elevator operated normally this time and she exited on the first floor.

"Help me, someone! Please, oh please, help me get out of here!"

Pat ran to the big bay window in the waiting room. She grabbed a floor lamp and was about to smash it through the window.

Suddenly, a finely dressed man in an elegant suit responded, "Pat, that simply won't do."

He smiled at her. She cringed.

CHAPTER 14
JAY ROKER

The freezing cold was getting to Jay. The sidewalk counselors seemed to be warm enough, but he could barely feel his hands and feet. He decided to go into the clinic to warm up for ten minutes. He turned around and opened the clinic door. As he entered, he was surprised to see that Pat was not at her desk.

Removing his gloves, he started to rub his hands together. Though warmer than outside, it felt awfully cold in the clinic.

"Maybe something is wrong with the heating system," he thought.

Jay walked past the waiting room, but no one was there. He walked down the hallway. Glancing into the room where the accountant might be, he saw no one.

"Gee, this is odd."

He returned to the entrance, where the pathetic little Christmas tree was lit up. They put it up shortly after the Thanksgiving holiday. Jay noted that the manger scene was deliberately omitted.

"They shouldn't have put anything up! How can you have a Christmas tree without a manger scene? If Grandma Pearl ever saw this pathetic tree, she'd pick it up and fling it in the street," Jay thought.

He went back to the front doors of the clinic.

"Damn, I can't get warm today. Maybe one of those nice ladies outside will get me some coffee," he thought.

Jay attempted to open the door, but the knob didn't budge. Again and again, he tried to open the door without success.

"Man, this is the pits today!"

Moving away from the front door, Jay walked to the side door of the clinic, the one that Dr. Weiss used to avoid the sidewalk counselors. He depressed the panic bar, but the door didn't open. Jay began to wonder what was happening. He decided to go downstairs. Normally, he was not allowed to go where the abortions were performed, but there was a back door he could try there.

Pressing the elevator button, Jay descended a flight and found himself looking down a dimly lit corridor. He glanced around to see if anyone was around then proceeded to run down the corridor trying to avoid being discovered. The door did not budge. Jay was terrified.

"What the hell is going around here? Where did everyone go?"

No sooner had he said this when a tall man dressed in an elegant suit appeared by the elevator.

"Greetings and felicitations, Jay!"

"Who the hell are you? What's going on here?"

The gentleman gestured for Jay to accompany him. "I am your worst nightmare. Just follow me."

CHAPTER 15
DR. SAMUEL WEISS

By three o'clock, Sam was feeling tired and annoyed. Several of the girls had minor problems during the abortions, but they would all be fine. Some of them were veterans at having abortions. One girl had had four abortions.

"Why don't they just act responsibly and use birth control?" thought Sam.

But, on second thought, he noted the irony that by far the majority of patients at the abortion clinic were using contraceptives.

Earlier in his medical career, Sam had been a birth control advocate. He believed that no woman should have a child she didn't want. That made perfect sense. He began reading about the life of Margaret Sanger, who was the inspiration behind the organization called Planned Parenthood. He thought he would find in her a heroine for the cause of responsible parenthood, but what he discovered turned his stomach.

Like Adolf Hitler, Sanger had an agenda for minorities and the poor. Basically, she wanted to control the population of the undesirables, and even went so far as to propose that birth licenses be required for parenthood. Such practices would parallel the present system in China that prohibits more than one child per family.

Sanger's goals of promoting unrestricted sexual activity, contraception, abortion and eugenics were documented facts. The more Sam read about Sanger, the less he valued her agenda.

His mind wandered again. When Ethel found out she was pregnant with Helene, Sam wasn't overly enthusiastic.

"We could have waited another year or two," he told his wife.

Ethel protested, "Sammy, you're never satisfied with anyone or anything. I'm glad I'm pregnant. I want this child!"

Sam tried to smooth down his wife's feathers.

"I'm not saying I don't want this baby. I'm just commenting that another year or two would have helped us out financially."

He remembered Ethel ignoring his words.

"If it's a girl, I want her to be named after my grandmother, Helene."

"Whatever you want, dear," Sam responded.

Ethel usually got what she wanted, and she was usually right. This time was no exception. If the truth be told, he was glad that Helene was born. Following Helene's birth, Ethel suffered two miscarriages. Helene was their only child, and Sam doted on her. A profound sadness enveloped Sam as he remembered the image of his daughter's body lying in her coffin.

Before Sam moved into the next room to perform another abortion, he felt the most intense chill go through his entire body. His fingers felt frozen. The door slammed shut.

"What the heck!"

He noticed that the room was empty. He went over to the door and tried to open it. Over and over, he turned the knob. Knocking loudly and calling out to the nurse, his voice became hoarse and his knuckles became sore. He tried to use the intercom, but it was dead. Standing back from the door, he looked around the room.

"No windows," he thought. "I'm trapped!"

The door opened slowly. Standing in the doorway was a finely attired man wearing an expensive gold wristwatch and a diamond lapel pin that appeared to have an inverted cross.

"Well, Samuel, it's good to see you. Follow me!"

"Who are you? What's going on! I'm calling the police!"

"Oh, Samuel, the police can't help you. No one can. Follow me and don't get me angry."

Sam stood at attention. Something or someone pushed him forward, and he followed the man.

Chapter 16
Shelley DeSimone

Shelley arrived at her apartment on the north side of Indianapolis. As she walked toward her condominium, she passed her neighbor, Cathy, and her Labradoodle named Chocolate. Shelley and Cathy jogged together on weekends with Chocolate. She was crazy about the dog, but was oblivious to the animal less than twenty feet away from her.

Chocolate was jumping wildly, waiting for Shelley to greet him. Cathy was stunned as Shelley ignored them both. As she arrived at her door, her neighbor, Frank Ford, a retired pharmacist, was exiting his condo. Shelley was unaware that tears were pouring down her face.

Frank called out to her.

"Shelley, are you all right?"

Shelley glanced in his direction.

"I'm fine, Mr. Ford."

He watched Shelley as she slammed her apartment door shut. She threw her coat on the floor and walked directly to her bedroom. She gazed down at her bed with its rose-colored quilt. She had shared this bed with Mark only weeks ago. Now everything was over.

Shelley's eyes traveled around her exquisitely decorated and furnished bedroom. Her job in the legal field had earned her enough money to buy the best in contemporary furnishings for her apartment. Standing before a full-length mirror, Shelley stared at her disheveled auburn hair and hazel eyes that looked back at her with indifference.

Walking over to her night table, she searched for a bottle of sleeping pills. Sitting on the edge of her bed, she examined the contents of the plastic bottle.

"Nearly full."

She went into the bathroom and filled a glass of water. Returning to her bedroom, she began taking three pills at a time until the bottle was empty.

As Shelly gulped the last three pills, her eyes moved around the room. She rose from the bed and walked toward a picture of her parents on their thirty-fifth wedding anniversary. Rosemary and Matthew DeSimone looked radiant. Her eyes filled with tears.

Her mother had been her lifeline until one year ago when she died of leukemia, right before Shelly's twenty-eighth birthday. Matt DeSimone had died five years earlier of lung cancer. Holding the photo, she drew it to her heart.

Shelley's imagination took her to Castleton Square Mall and to the image of Mark, Laura and their two children strolling through the maze of people. She had spotted them by accident. Mark was holding his son in his arms as his wife walked hand in hand with their oldest son, Mark Jr., who was no more than 5 years old.

As she cried, she could hear a voice within her.

"Shelley, he was married. He was never yours."

"But I loved him . . . I loved him . . ."

Holding the wedding photo of her parents, she laid down on her bed. She thought back to her childhood. Her parents wanted children so badly, but were unable to conceive. They were overjoyed when St. Elizabeth's Home called to confirm that they would be able to adopt a newborn girl who had been placed for adoption by a 15-year-old unwed mother.

Michelle was the name that her teenage birth mother had given her. Rosemary decided to keep the name as a way of honoring the girl who made a loving choice for her baby.

"Shelley, abortion was legal when your mother became pregnant. She was only fifteen years old when she decided to give you life."

Her mother went on to explain that her birth mother, Amber, was being pressured to abort her baby by her boyfriend and even by her parents. Amber turned to a faculty member at Cardinal Ritter High School for guidance. She and her family were then led to St. Elizabeth's Home. It was there that she decided in favor of adoption.

When she was a teenager, Shelley's parents gave her a handwritten letter composed by her birth mother. She treasured it, and memorized some of the paragraphs:

Michelle,

I want you to know that I love you, and I always will love you. I know I can't give you the kind of life you deserve. This is a big sacrifice to give you up, but I know I'm doing the right thing for both of us.

I could never have aborted you like people told me to. I want you to live even if it means without me.

Have a great life, Michelle. If you ever think about me, say a little prayer. I'll never forget you or stop loving you.

Though she had never met her birth mother, each year on her birthday Shelley and her parents attended a Mass for her at their parish church.

Shelley's mind returned to Mark.

"Why, Mark? Why did it have to end like this?"

"Shelley, he was never yours! Love doesn't steal from another. Love never destroys."

This time she recognized the voice of her mother.

"Michelle, suicide is a mortal sin!"

Now it was her father's voice that she heard. He always used her full name when he reprimanded her as a child. It startled her. In an instant, Shelley feared death, feared going to hell because she was committing suicide. She regretted taking the pills.

"What was I thinking? Adultery! Suicide! I need to stay awake!!"

She attempted to get out of bed and move toward her telephone on the desk to call for help. The room disappeared around her, and then there was total blackness.

CHAPTER 17
NICK TROIANO
AND LARRY KLEIN

Nick and Larry talked about insignificant things as the limousine sped down the Belt Parkway. Nick began to question Larry about his party loyalties in the next presidential election.

"No kidding. You're an Independent? I figured you for a Democrat. Most Jews are Democrats."

Larry smiled uncomfortably.

"Now, me, I'm a Democrat turned Republican. Those Democrats support gay marriage and the likes. What is this country coming to?"

"Imagine, the man is talking about values and lives the life of a ruthless barbarian!" Larry thought as he considered Nick's drug trade, loan sharking, embezzlements and murders.

Larry often regretted his introduction to the Troiano family ten years before. His gambling debts led him to Nick, who in turn offered him a way out of his problems if he would help the family from time to time. It was like sliding down a slippery slope until he reached the bottom of the pit, where he was presently located.

Larry's commitments to this vile man and his criminal family were instrumental in destroying his fifteen-year marriage to Doris. His frequent late-night excursions to meet with "clients," his inability to tell the truth when questioned about his legal practices, his refusal to resign as an attorney for the Troiano family when friends and family pleaded with him, and his growing abuse of alcohol and irrational behavior ultimately destroyed his relationship with his wife and his twin sons, Jacob and Joel.

Larry gulped his whiskey, poured himself another glass and adjusted his fine gray silk tie, then leaned over to whisper to Nick.

"Well, Boss, some of your family members should consider going into politics to clean things up."

"Larry, I was thinking the same thing. Actually, my brother's son is a lawyer and he has expressed some political ambitions. I'd back him in a minute."

Larry trembled at the idea of one of the Troianos going into politics. He knew firsthand how evil Nick and his brothers were. He felt sick to his stomach at how evil he had become. As he smiled at Nick, he saw his own reflection in Nick's sunglasses that rested on the portable bar. He gazed at his graying hair and receding hairline. His thin face revealed a sharp hooked nose that Nick often kidded Larry about.

"You could use that nose like a weapon if you needed to!" Nick had told him.

Larry's facial expression definitely revealed a broken and desperate man. Larry's father often said to his children, "When you hang around with dogs, you're bound to get fleas."

How he had wished to liberate himself from this dog!

Suddenly, out of nowhere, a car swerved out of control and crossed over into their lane. He could hear the sound of metal screeching. The crash happened in a few split seconds. Nick, Larry and the chauffeur were unconscious as emergency medical technicians in ambulances rushed to the site of the accident. The driver of the other vehicle, a man in his late sixties, had suffered a fatal heart attack at the wheel. He was pronounced dead at the scene.

CHAPTER 18
MICHAEL REID AND
SISTER MARY GRACE DONNELLAN

Michael Reid entered his small office in James Hall. He opened his notes for the interview with Sister Mary Grace Donnellan. Before he began perusing his notes, he walked over to his closet. There was a mirror mounted on the door. He was pleased with his appearance. He adjusted his red pullover sweater and rubbed his hands together, trying to restore some circulation to them.

Returning to his desk, he opened a folder. He wanted to make sure he covered all the bases and asked the proper questions about death, dying and the faith experience.

Michael was going to interview this 75-five-year-old nun who was dying of cancer. She agreed to the interview after her grandniece, Beth, a student in Reid's class, set up the appointment.

In advance, he told her that his interview was designed to show that Christianity satisfies the human need to make sense out of dying.

What he didn't tell her was that he was going to argue in his book that psychotherapeutic drugs achieved better results in helping people accept the inevitability of death. He would argue that death is an unfortunate consequence of life. In his book, he would advocate euthanasia and assisted suicide as the humane way to bring life to a dignified end. He would propose that religion simply complicates the death process, which should be as painless and as quick as possible.

As Michael thought about Sister Mary Grace, a retired English teacher at Immaculata High School in Bay Ridge, his mind traveled back to his own senior year at Bishop Ford High School in Brooklyn, the same year his parents were in the throes of a nasty divorce.

Michael had felt as though his world was falling apart when his father walked out of their lives and moved to Florida to find out who he really was. Allan Reid was a very self-absorbed man and did not calculate that his journey to self-discovery would destroy a family. Instead of finding out who he really was, he found a younger wife and another ready-made family. Within ten years, he was married three times and divorced three times.

During the first year of his divorce from Michael's mother, Allan invited his son to visit with his new family in Florida. Buoyed by the possibility of sharing quality time with his father, Michael jumped at the opportunity.

The brief stay with his father and stepfamily proved to be disastrous. Michael found himself constantly fighting with his younger stepbrother. Allan's wife accused Michael of being the cause of dissension in the house. She warned him that he would not be welcome to return for visits if he persisted in his behavior.

Ultimately, Michael found himself at serious odds with his own father over his stepmother's son. To Michael's chagrin, his father took the side of this adolescent terror, who was a master at manipulation and control. Michael vowed never to return for a visit, and he made good on his pledge.

Gradually, the telephone calls between Michael and his father became more infrequent and his relationship with his father was reduced to a few greeting cards sent during the year and at Christmas.

By his sophomore year in college, Michael, like his father, wanted to find himself. But instead of finding himself, he indulged himself in sinful pleasures that were easily obtainable in the immoral climate of a secular college campus. He was also attracted to theories about life that were devoid of any supernatural values. His life was on a steady moral decline by age 19.

CHAPTER 19
DENISE SMITH

Be sober, be watchful. Your adversary the devil prowls around like a roaring lion, seeking some one to devour. Resist him, firm in your faith, knowing that the same experience of suffering is required of your brotherhood throughout the world.

(1 Peter 5:8–9)

Wearing only her hospital gown, Denise stood before the elegantly dressed man. She felt naked and vulnerable.

"Please help me," she pleaded. "I don't know where everyone is. I just need to find my clothes and get out of here."

"Denise, Denise. There is no way out. Oh, how rude of me. Let me introduce myself. I am an angel."

"An angel? What do you mean? Angels are supposed to help people!"

Denise noticed his inverted diamond cross and gold wristwatch with no hands.

"Ah, yes. Your guardian angel attempted to help you. You ignored that poor fool. I am an angel, though a fallen one. My name is Lucifer. You may call me Satan or, better yet, refer to me as Master!"

Denise was filled with terror and began shaking violently.

"You are not my Master. Jesus is my Lord."

Suddenly, she felt herself thrown against the walls repeatedly. Her shoulders ached from the pain as she regained her balance.

"Let's get something straight, my little pet. You are never to use that name in my presence. It is blasphemy!"

"I don't want to be here. I'm sorry for having the abortion. I had no choice!"

"Really!" Satan laughed. "Get on that elevator. I want to give you a tour of your future dwelling place."

Glancing at his wristwatch, Satan laughed.

"This is the only wristwatch that has no hands! Time stands still where you are going, my pet."

"No! Leave me alone!"

Denise made the sign of the cross.

Satan turned to Denise.

"This isn't some vampire movie, you know, although we do have some real bloodsuckers down here! Stop your foolishness and follow me."

Feeling herself pushed into the elevator, Denise prayed silently in her heart.

"I hear your feeble prayers. It's too late, Denise. It's much too late for you. Prepare yourself for eternity!"

Denise's mind raced.

"How do I get out of here? Is it possible I died during the procedure? Oh, Jesus, help me!!"

Satan responded with a terrifying voice.

"I warned you about using that name."

The doors of the elevator parted and two young children greeted Denise. At least they appeared to be children. They laughed maliciously as they grabbed at her hospital gown.

"Get away from me!"

To her surprise, the two children were actually demons. Both were less than four feet tall and had large black eyes and rotting fang-like teeth. They looked like something out of a horror movie. They reached for her and began kicking and punching her to the ground.

Denise tried to protect herself against their vicious attacks. She was terrified beyond words.

"That's enough, boys. You have all eternity to play with her," Satan said, laughing.

The demons retreated reluctantly, but not before one of them bit her arm and drew blood. Denise rose to her feet, weeping and in pain.

"Come, my dear, the adventure is only beginning!"

CHAPTER 20
JAY ROKER

Lord, thou hast been our dwelling place in all genera-
tions. Before the mountains were brought forth, or ever
thou hadst formed the earth and the world, from everlast-
ing to everlasting thou art God. Thou turnest man back to
the dust, and sayest, "Turn back, O children of men!" For
a thousand years in thy sight are but as yesterday when
it is past, or as a watch in the night. Thou dost sweep
men away; they are like a dream, like grass which is re-
newed in the morning: in the morning it flourishes and is
renewed; in the evening it fades and withers.
(Psalm 90:1–6)

Jay followed the gentleman in the fine tailored blue-pinstriped suit. He noticed his gold cuff links with bold crosses upside down. His diamond lapel pin with the upside-down cross and wristwatch with no hands also drew Jay's attention.

"Jay, you're a smart dude. I'm sure you've figured all this out already."

"What I've figured out is that I don't care for your jewelry, and I don't particularly care for you. I don't belong here!"

"Oh, Jackson Roker, you most certainly do belong here. What makes you think you're different from all my other guests?"

"What did I ever do that was wrong? Yeah, I made some mistakes."

"No, Jackson Roker, you sinned grievously throughout your life. I'm not complaining though! Actually, it gives me great pleasure to know all your weaknesses. I was behind those nasty sins you committed in high school and college."

Satan elbowed him as he said this and raised his eyebrows as if to be humorous.

"I was even behind your sister's abortion."

"Hey, wait a minute. She never did have that abortion!"

"Correct. Your grandmother, Pearl, was a Baptist prayer warrior. She constantly prayed for her children and grandchildren. Her prayers were like acid falling on ice!"

"I wish she had prayed as hard for me!"

Satan laughed.

"Even Grandma Pearl's prayers can't save you now, Jay. Resign yourself to all of this."

"I'll never resign myself to this," Jay thought silently.

"Oh, Jay, I can read your thoughts. Read the sign above the door, please. Read it in a nice loud voice."

Jay shivered. The sign read: "No happiness, no peace and no rest for those who enter, for ages unending."

"Welcome to your new home, Jay!"

Satan laughed loudly. He pushed Jay through the doorway with a simple thought.

CHAPTER 21
PAT MARINO

For we are consumed by thy anger; by thy wrath we are overwhelmed. Thou hast set our iniquities before thee, our secret sins in the light of thy countenance.

(Psalm 90:7–8)

Satan faced Pat as she was poised to throw a floor lamp through the window of the abortion clinic.

"Pat, my dear, there is no escape. You'll never be free again."

She watched as Satan walked toward her.

"Stay away from me!" Pat screamed.

"Is that any way for you to treat a friend? I am your friend, you know. I've been with you since you were fifteen years old. You gave yourself to me so totally and so freely. Don't you remember?"

"What are you talking about? I never met you."

"Think, Pat. The attic in Sheepshead Bay. You and your friends and the Ouiji Board."

"That was just a game!"

"Was it? You and your girlfriends seemed very serious about that 'game.' You called upon the spirits and you enjoyed the little dial moving telling you about your lives. You enjoyed that game, didn't you? Admit it, Patricia."

Pat remained silent.

She recalled the day that she, Stacey and Carol purchased the Ouiji Board. They hid it in her attic and only played the game when they were sure no one was around. It started off innocently enough.

"O.K., you start, Stacey. Ask it a question," said Pat.

"Will I graduate from high school with honors?"

The three of them laughed as Stacey posed the question, knowing that she barely pulled a C-plus average. The dial began to move beneath their hands. It indicated "NO."

Carol asked the next question.

"Will I marry Jeff after high school?"

Again, the dial moved and indicated "NO."

"You're not really disappointed, Carol, are you?" Pat asked.

"Not at all. I plan on breaking up with him. I just want to test this thing out."

"Let's get serious with our questions," Stacey interjected.

"Let me start," Carol broke in. "You know that my grandmother was admitted to the hospital a few days ago. She suffered a stroke. I'd really like to know if she's going to get better. The doctors are cautiously optimistic. Will my grandmother get better?"

The girls put their hands on the dial and the response was "NO."

Carol was visibly upset.

"If you creeps think this is funny, you're sick!"

Pat and Stacey assured Carol that they did not manipulate the dial. They all took a deep breath.

"O.K. Is my grandmother going to have to go to a nursing home?"

The dialed indicated "NO."

"Is she coming home to us?"

Again, the dial indicated "NO."

"Well, if she's not going to get better or go to a nursing home or come back home to us, then is she going to die?"

The dial spelled "YES."

"Let's stop this game," Pat insisted. "It's no fun anymore."

"No, let's finish it! When is my grandmother going to die?"

They all hesitated, but put their hands on the dial. It spelled out "T O N I G H T."

The three of them gasped. With their hands still fixed on the dial, it began to move again. As it moved from letter to letter, they read out loud, "FRIENDSFOREVERANDEVER."

Carol drew back her hand from the dial.

"This is no game. Did we ever stop to think who might be sending us these messages?"

"I doubt it is Casper the friendly ghost!" added Stacey.

Pat picked up the Ouiji Board and put it back inside the suitcase, where it was hidden in the attic.

"Whose idea was it anyway to buy this stupid game?"

Stacey and Carol yelled back, "Yours!!"

That evening, Carol's mother received a call from the hospital. It was approximately nine o'clock when her mother's condition deteriorated. She and her husband went to the hospital. Around ten-thirty, Carol's father called home with the news that their grandmother had passed away peacefully. Carol ran to her room and called Stacey and Pat with the sad news.

It wasn't until after the funeral that Carol confided to her mother that she, Pat and Stacey had known about their grandmother's death through a message on the Ouiji Board.

Pat's parents were in a rage over it. Her father went to the attic and got the board then took it to the garage, where his wife and Pat stood beside him.

"This object has no place in our home!"

Taking his power saw, he cut the board into smaller pieces then doused it with lighter fluid and burned it in their gas barbeque grill.

"Young lady, you don't dabble with the occult! This was no game. You want to play a game, play Monopoly!"

Pat had never seen her father so angry at her before.

Satan could read Pat's thoughts.

"Pat, that last message, before your dear father destroyed the board, was from me to you. 'Friends forever and ever.' I like to keep my promises."

Then Satan continued with all formality, "Then, of course, you started to delve into Wicca in college. You and your friends thought it was so cool to get in touch with the 'feminine side of the deity.' You prayed to all those charming little goddesses. Did you know that the demons so enjoyed your acts of worship?"

"They were all harmless games."

"Yes, Pat. Then why did you hide those harmless games from your parents? They were games, supernatural games, and you lost all of them. You lost everything and forever. But not all is lost. You gained me!"

Then looking Pat straight in the eye, Satan asked, "But you know what really made you a loser?"

Pat looked away from Satan, afraid of the answer.

"Ah, come on, Pat. You know what you did! Sometimes abortion backfires on me, but not in your case. Women will have one or two or more then repent. But you, my dear, never repented! You dug your little heels into the ground and felt justified in your decision. After all, Paul wanted nothing to do with you and the child."

Satan smiled at Pat.

"You even took the job at the Caring Clinic for Women. You see those arches outside the front door? They are invisible gates, gates to my kingdom. Exactly

125 women have had abortions because of your advice and encouragement as the receptionist there. You calmed the fears and numbed the consciences of so many women. You were an excellent promoter. There's certainly a place for you in my kingdom."

Pat reeled from the idea of spending eternity in hell.

"If I could relive my life, I would repent. I would reject you and all that you stand for."

"Let's not get vulgar, Pat. You had your opportunity to repent. Now you're mine, completely and forever."

Satan smiled again and extended his hand to Pat. She refused to take it. He reached out and grabbed her arm. She noticed his claw-like nails and the expensive watch without hands.

"Come with me, and don't resist."

Pat wept bitterly. She wanted to escape from this fiend and could find no way to do so.

CHAPTER 22
MAGGIE AND JOHN SMITH

So teach us to number our days that we may get a heart of wisdom.

(Psalm 90:12)

Margaret Smith, "Maggie" to her friends, wondered about her daughter's unusual behavior during the past couple of weeks. John, her husband of twenty-eight years, walked into the kitchen.

"John, I have a real bad feeling about Denise."

"Ah, you and your feelings," muttered John.

"No, John, listen to me. Ever since Denise started dating Greg, she's changed. She's been avoiding me for weeks."

"That's because you're noisy, Maggie. Cut her some slack, will ya?"

"John, the other day, when I was cleaning Denise's bedroom, I found a piece of paper with an address on it. It's the address of the Caring Clinic for Women."

"What the heck is the Caring Clinic for Women?"

"It's an abortion clinic."

John straightened up.

"Is it possible she's pregnant? Dear God!"

"Before you get crazy, let's put our heads together on this. Do you think she told Brenda?"

"Where is she? Let's settle this matter."

"John, we've been married for twenty-eight years. You're a hotheaded Irishman. Please, John, sit down with me and let's talk this through. If Denise is considering an abortion, she's lost her way. I knew when she stopped going to church that we'd have problems. Sit down, honey. Let's figure this out."

John loved Maggie with all his heart. She was the anchor of the family and her deep faith was unquestionable.

"O.K., Maggie. We'll do it your way. We'll talk to her when she wakes up. But when all is said and done, I just want five minutes with that Greg."

CHAPTER 23
SHELLEY DeSIMONE

Hear, O Lord, when I cry aloud, be gracious to me and answer me! Thou hast said, "Seek ye my face." My heart says to thee, "Thy face, Lord, do I seek."
(Psalm 27:7–8)

Shelley lay motionless on her bed. She was aware of the fact that she was in bed, but was powerless to move. She desperately tried to open her eyes, but they remained tightly shut. A few times in her life, she had dreamed that she was asleep and unable to wake up. This experience was similar.

She felt a cold presence in the room. This presence made her feel uncomfortable and fearful. She wanted to wake up and get away. Then, suddenly, she sensed something different. She smelled perfume; it was her mother's perfume!

"Shelley, what have you done to yourself?"

She felt warmth all around her.

"Your mother and I are here."

It was her father's voice.

"Shelley, we are here to keep you awake."

"Mom, can you hear me? Daddy, can you hear me?"

Shelley was unable to speak and could only communicate with her mind.

"Your mother and I can hear you. So can God."

"I'm not ready to die. I'm sorry I took the pills. I was out of my mind with grief. I wanted the pain to go away."

"Shelley, adultery is a mortal sin and so is suicide. Before we arrived, Satan was standing by your bed, hovering over you like a beast of prey ready to devour you."

"Mother, I'm scared. I want to open my eyes to look at you and Daddy. I can't see or move."

"Shelley, remember us as we were. Find us in your heart. Can you see us?"

"Yes. I see the two of you standing at the foot of my bed."

The image of her parents consoled her. They appeared as they did in their thirty-fifth wedding anniversary picture. Her father was bald with just a crown of gray hair encircling his head. He was in his fine black suit and blue tie. Her mother had her gray hair styled in a chignon. She appeared in her cream-colored gown that was topped with a short matching jacket. A string of pearls complimented her attire.

"Now, listen to us, Michelle. You have only a few moments left to make things right with God. If you should die unrepentant, you'll belong to that dreadful creature for all eternity. Is that what you want?"

"Your father and I adopted you for this life and the next. We want you with us forever in heaven. Even your birth mother knew that you belonged to God when she conceived you. You were not brought into this world to be lost forever."

"I want to go to heaven."

"Michelle, you must have perfect contrition for your sins. That means you must love God sincerely and truly repent of your sins. Whatever happens in the next few minutes, remember that we love you."

"I don't want to die."

"It's all in God's merciful hands now, Shelley."

CHAPTER 24
DENISE SMITH

Hear the voice of my supplication, as I cry to thee for help,
as I lift up my hands toward thy most holy sanctuary.
(Psalm 28:2)

As the doors of the elevator opened, Satan turned to Denise in disgust.

"You stay here for now."

He exited the elevator and the door closed tightly. From outside the elevator, she heard Satan yell back, "There's no hope for you, Denise Maria Goretti Smith! You're mine! Nobody can pray you out of here. No one!"

Denise pressed the elevator button to the first floor. As she wiped the tears from her eyes, the door opened again. She stepped out on the first floor and ran to the windows in the waiting area. As she peered through the blinds, she saw some older women and men praying the rosary.

"If only I had listened to my conscience."

Denise began to feel some warmth in her body again. She couldn't hear the people outside, but somehow their presence comforted her.

She banged on the windows to no avail. She went over to the door and tried the knob, but it was still locked.

"I don't want to be lost forever."

Denise went back into the waiting room and sat down.

"People who go to hell can't have hope. I do have hope! I want a second chance!"

Denise got up again and went over to the window to watch the sidewalk counselors. She knelt down on the floor, and made the sign of the cross.

"St. Maria. Please help me. You forgave the rapist who killed you. You even appeared to him in prison. He was even converted in prison. Please, help me now!"

Then Denise began to recite the Act of Contrition. She started the prayer over and over again, hoping to remember all the words. It had been so long since her last confession, and she couldn't remember the entire prayer.

Frustrated with herself, she cried out, "Forgive me, Lord!"

"Denise, do you want to go to confession?"

Denise turned around and saw Father Raymond Kassebart standing at the entrance to the waiting room.

Denise stood up. She picked up the sheet that fallen to the ground earlier and instinctively covered herself with it.

"Father, didn't you die a few years ago?"

"Yes, Denise. You were away at school at the time. I've been summoned to help you."

"Who sent you? Is this some kind of trick?"

"No, Denise. This is no trick. Didn't you just pray to St. Maria Goretti for help? Well, having been the priest who baptized you and gave you your first Holy Communion, she asked me to visit you. I'm here because your soul is in jeopardy. You violated your conscience; you knew what was right and wrong. You chose yourself over the life of your child. Your parents and countless people are praying for you. You are not lost yet. That's why that old devil abandoned you on the elevator. The prayers were too powerful for him. Right now, he's powerless in your regard, at least for the moment. But he will be back. I can assure you of that!"

"Oh, Father, please help me get out of here!"

"I am powerless to release you from this place. The power is within you."

Looking intently at Denise, he said, "What you wish to do?"

"Father, I want to go to confession. Can a dead priest hear confessions? Is it valid or lawful?"

"Stop thinking like a lawyer. The law exists only in time. You are beyond time, as we speak. Your salvation is hanging by a thread."

Father Kassebart gestured to two chairs.

"Come on, Denise. God's mercy awaits you. You have no time to lose."

As Denise began her confession to Father Kassebart, she realized that her decision to stop going to Mass on Sundays was the beginning of her spiritual death. For the longest time, her parents pressured her to continue going to Mass, but eventually they threw up their hands in despair. She won, or so she thought.

When Denise completed her confession, Father Kassebart raised his hand in absolution over her. Denise signed herself with the cross.

"Denise, you rebelled against God's moral laws. Now you've come back to your senses. Don't let that devil trip you up again!"

Father Kassebart rose from his seat and began to leave the room.

"Father, don't go! Please, don't leave me alone here!"

"Denise, you are never alone. Satan was correct when he told you that your guardian angel was trying to help you. Look to your left."

Standing some ten feet from her was what appeared to be an 8-year-old child. He wore something resembling a long white robe. A golden light encircled him. He bowed to her.

"My guardian angel?"

"Yes, Denise. He will remain with you until the final choice."

Suddenly, Father Kassebart and the angel disappeared.

"Oh, no, don't go! Please, please stay."

As Denise stood in the middle of the room, she prayed. It was as though the words had been suggested to her.

"Out of the depths, I cry to you. Lord, hear my prayer."

Chapter 25
Jay Roker and Grandma Pearl

O Lord, rebuke me not in thy anger, nor chasten me in thy wrath! For thy arrows have sunk into me, and thy hand has come down on me. There is no soundness in my flesh because of thy indignation; there is no health in my bones because of my sin. For my iniquities have gone over my head; they weigh like a burden too heavy for me. My wounds grow foul and fester because of my foolishness.
(Psalm 38:1–5)

Satan adjusted his shirtsleeves with annoyance. Pulling down on his vest, he hissed his way to the ante-chamber of hell.

"We'll see who wins this time."

Jay sat on the edge of a rock looking down into a great black abyss. Tortured screams could be heard rising from the depths. Pitiful moaning and curses filled the dank, cold air in this cave-like environment. There was a distinct stench, like rotting flesh.

"So, what do you think of the accommodations, Jay?"

Jay rose to his feet and ignored the question.

"I don't know much about anything, but I do admit that I sinned during my life. And yes, I broke just about all the Commandments. But, you know something, I still believe in Jesus. I was saved a long time ago! I shouldn't be here."

Satan's face grew more sinister.

"Don't ever mention that name in my presence again!"

As Satan said this, Jay was flung backward and landed on his side some fifteen feet away.

"How little you understand! Jay, my friend, you used your free will to welcome me into your life! You chose to reign with me! You know, I have an excellent memory. You once said, 'I'd rather rule in hell rather than serve in heaven.'"

Jay choked back tears, "Yeah, but I was just kidding with my friends! I was horsing around. Listen, I know I am a sinner. But now I want to be saved! I'm sorry . . ."

"Jackson, Jackson. You are not sorry for your sins. You are sorry you are here. There's a big difference. This is a done deal."

"No, I'm truly sorry for my sins, for each and every one of them. If I could start all over, I would choose Jesus and salvation."

Again, Satan flung Jay up against the rocks. The sharp edges of the rocks pierced Jay's back and sides. He knew he was bleeding.

With great pain, Jay chose to kneel on the rocky surface. As he did so, he remembered his Grandma Pearl telling him that the good Lord was scourged at the pillar for our sins. He accepted those stripes for all our sins.

"Lord Jesus, I choose you as my personal Lord and Savior. Forgive me for all the wrong I've done in my life. Help me out of the dark pit I find myself in."

Suddenly, Jay found himself on the first floor of the abortion clinic. It was dark and no one else was around. Then he heard a familiar voice.

"Jay, come to Grandma."

She motioned for him to join her in the waiting room. She was wearing her Sunday best. Grandma Pearl had few outfits in her wardrobe. Her best outfits were reserved for Sundays. She had insisted on being buried in her light-green suit and her straw hat with the pink rosebuds that trimmed it.

"I want to look my best as I cross over from this life to the next," insisted Grandma Pearl. "Make sure you bury me in my Easter outfit, the light-green suit and my hat with the rosebuds."

"Grandma, how did you get here? Is this a trick?"

"Jay, this is Grandma Pearl. Now, you listen to me boy. Sit down. Your salvation is the reason I'm here. I've been watching over you and your sisters. The good Lord wants all of you saved, but you and your sisters have followed the ways of the world. And you, all those vile sins you've committed. Working for an abortion clinic, no less! Lord, have mercy! I wanted to throttle you every day you came to this disgusting place."

"Granny, what's going to happen to me? Can you help me?"

"Grandma Pearl would never abandon you. I was just talking to Mary. You know, Jesus' mother. And she said, 'Pearl, you go and get our boy and make sure he comes home to us.'"

"Oh, Granny, I'll do whatever it takes to get out of here."

"Jay, it's not going to be easy. Are you willing to do everything it takes?"

"Everything!"

"Then you listen up, Jackson. Do as I tell you."

CHAPTER 26
MICHAEL REID AND SISTER MARY GRACE DONNELLAN

As a hart [deer] longs for flowing streams, so longs my soul for thee, O God. My soul thirsts for God, for the living God. When shall I come and behold the face of God? My tears have been my food day and night, while men say to me continually, "Where is your God?"

(Psalm 42:1–3)

Michael Reid was startled by a knock on his office door. Putting his silver-rimmed glasses back on, he sat up in his chair.

"Who is it?"

"It's Sister Mary Grace. May I come in?"

"Sister Mary Grace?"

Opening the door, he looked down at a petite 75-year-old nun. She wore a simple navy blue habit and black veil. She decided against wearing street clothes in the 1970s when the community members opted for secular clothing. She was criticized for her decision to continue wearing the modified habit, but their words were like water off a duck's back.

"I didn't expect to see a Sister in a habit!"

"I didn't expect to see such a handsome professor!"

Michael Reid actually blushed at Sister Mary Grace's comment.

"But don't let your good looks go to your head. God looks into the heart. That is where true beauty resides, and that's where it counts. And you can't see it in that mirror over there."

"You're a feisty nun! Did I miss something in my communications with your grandniece about our appointment? I thought I was to visit you tomorrow at your convent for the interview."

"You didn't miss a thing, Professor Reid. As it turns out, I have another pressing commitment tomorrow. I decided to visit you today, if that is convenient for you."

Michael Reid eyed the nun. For someone dying from cancer, she appeared fairly spry.

"Please come in, Sister Mary Grace. I do, in fact, have some time to interview you."

Sister Mary Grace smiled.

"I'm sure you won't be disappointed by this interview."

"Please, have a seat. How are you feeling?"

"I'm doing well."

"Did a companion bring you?"

Michael couldn't believe she had come alone. He glanced down the hallway to look for her companion.

Sister Mary Grace smiled.

"I am always companioned. Why don't we get down to the business at hand? My companion will return for me when we are finished with our business."

Michael reached for a tape recorder and, looking up, asked, "Do you mind if I tape our conversation?"

"Please do."

Reaching for his notes and a legal pad, he began to question the elderly nun who had only weeks to live. He had gathered all the necessary facts about her from her grandniece, Beth.

"Sister, how long have you been in religious life?"

"Fifty-seven years. I entered right out of high school."

"Was religion always an important part of your life?"

"Most definitely. My parents were very devout Catholics. They came over from the old country—Ireland, that is. I am one of five children, the only girl. They raised us with traditional Catholic values and beliefs."

"So, you've always been a practicing Catholic?"

"Yes, sir."

"Beth, your grandniece, told me that you've been diagnosed with terminal cancer."

Michael cleared his throat, knowing that he was about to ask the difficult questions.

"Professor, you want to know my feelings about facing death and how my faith prepares me for it."

Relieved that she was so easy to interview, Michael responded, "Yes, please address that. And call me Michael."

"Michael, death is an inevitable part of life. Our American culture tries to avoid any serious discussion about death. It is a scary thing. What we know is that life ends and what lies ahead is unknown or known only through faith. For those who have faith, death is the door to eternal life with God. I want to share with you my recent death experience because I want you to believe again."

Michael looked up from his writing pad, puzzled.

"What do you mean your 'recent death experience?' You talk about death as though it were an accomplished fact."

Sister Mary Grace looked into Michael's light gray eyes and smiled.

"May I continue? It will become clear to you in a few moments."

Michael nodded.

"This morning, I was sitting in my wheelchair by my bedroom window. I was watching the birds carrying twigs and blades of grass to their nest in a nearby tree. Watching the birds make their nest made me recall that this Earth is only a temporary nest or dwelling place for us. Our real dwelling place is in heaven.

"I felt a longing in my heart for that eternal dwelling place where God reigns. Suddenly, I turned to the door as I heard a rustling sound. A beautiful woman entered the room. I knew it was the Blessed Mother. She smiled at me. I knew she came for me."

Michael flipped his pen down. He thought to himself that this elderly nun was a little nuts, and that his interview was being wasted. Maybe she wasn't even dying of cancer. Not wanting to be rude, he allowed her to continue.

"I felt a surge of energy enter into my body one last time. I rose from my wheelchair and walked toward this beautiful woman dressed in white and beige. She gestured for me to follow her to the chapel.

"Michael, death was not a frightening experience for me once I realized to whom I was going. I entered the chapel and immediately fell upon my knees in adoration. The Lord smiled at me and lifted me up from the floor. My soul was immediately judged in his presence. All the sins of my life were clearly before me. My sorrow for all my sins was so intense that I could barely remain standing. The gaze of the Lord was purifying me. Then the Lord told me that I would be with him in heaven forever. He had prepared my dwelling place with him."

Michael moved about in his seat with impatience.

Sister Mary Grace looked at him.

"Rewind your tape recorder, and play it."

Michael did as she commanded. He pressed the play button. What he heard back left him speechless.

CHAPTER 27
DR. SAMUEL WEISS AND HELENE WEISS

For evils have encompassed me without number; my iniquities have overtaken me, till I cannot see; they are more than the hairs of my head; my heart fails me. Be pleased, O Lord, to deliver me! O Lord, make haste to help me!
(Psalm 40:12–13)

Sam found himself sitting in what appeared to be an operating room. Satan stood by the table with all kinds of instruments neatly placed on top of white cloth.

"Great instruments these are, Sammy."

Satan lifted each of the instruments used routinely during abortions.

"This one cuts up the babies, and this one vacuums them out."

"Stop it. I know what each instrument does."

"So, you freely chose to destroy children in their mothers' wombs? Most people try to rationalize their way out of abortion. What I like about you is that you call a spade a spade! You know, Sammy, I think abortion is a great thing."

Satan had Sam's attention.

"I knew this would interest you, Sam. I have a great investment in the abortion industry. With each abortion, I strike at my enemy. Every pathetic human life is made in the image and likeness of my opponent. For the time being, I can't hurt him directly, so I destroy what he loves."

Sam looked up. Trying to avoid the name of God, he asked, "Why do you hate him so much?"

"I hate him because he's weak. I am stronger and more powerful. Look at the world. It's mine! It's all mine! You're mine! People obey and worship me!"

As Sam watched Satan fill with pride, he remembered a verse from the Book of Deuteronomy, "Choose life that you may live."

"What are you thinking, Sammy boy? I am an expert in the Scriptures. I can quote them freely. You can't choose life. After all, you've chosen death for the past twenty-four years! Your fate is sealed. Don't waste time thinking frivolous thoughts."

Sam paused before answering.

"I'm not thinking frivolous thoughts. He is the one who gives life. I choose to follow him, not you!"

In an instant, Sam felt catapulted through a long tunnel. He found himself again on the first floor of the clinic. Standing in his little office, he began to shake and sob.

As he struggled to regain his composure, he noticed his daughter, Helene, smiling at him. She appeared as she was before her tragic death. Her long, dark-brown hair fell loosely to her waist. She wore the clothes she was buried in, a yellow blouse and pantsuit that were purchased for the eleventh birthday she never celebrated. He noticed the little charm bracelet that he and his wife had bought for her. That, too, was buried with her.

"Daddy, I'm here. Don't be afraid. I want to help you."

"Helene, my dear child. How can you help me?"

"I was sent to teach you the way back. Uncle Bernie and I knew that you needed us."

"Uncle Bernie?"

"Yes. He thought it was best for me to come to you. He prays for you all the time."

"But, Uncle Bernie is . . ."

" . . . retarded. He was retarded on Earth, but in heaven there is only perfection. He has received all good things from the giver of all good things. Sickness, handicaps and other such things do not exist in the heavenly kingdom. In the physical world that is locked in time and space, these things exist because of original sin. Earlier you quoted from the Book of Deuteronomy. It is the Author of life who has restored all things to Uncle Bernie. It is the Lamb who has sent me to you. He wants to restore life to your soul."

"I don't understand. You mean God? You're speaking strangely to me."

Helene smiled.

"It will all become clear to you soon. Let me tell you what you need to do. Satan wants you very, very badly. It will take all your strength to fight him. Don't give in to him. Are you ready to fight him with all your will?"

"With every ounce of my strength, I will resist him."

CHAPTER 28
NICK TROIANO AND LARRY KLEIN

Behold, thou hast made my days a few handbreadths, and my lifetime is as nothing in thy sight. Surely every man stands as a mere breath! Surely man goes about as a shadow! Surely for nought are they in turmoil; man heaps up, and knows not who will gather! "And now, Lord, for what do I wait? My hope is in thee."

(Psalm 39:5–7)

Nick Troiano opened his eyes. He glanced over to where Larry had been sitting. He was slumped over in his seat. Blood was everywhere. Larry looked dead. Blood trickled from his hooked nose and head. The chauffeur was being strapped to a gurney then loaded into an ambulance. Nick started to knock on the window to get the attention of the police and paramedics at the scene.

"Hey, get me out of here!"

No one seemed to be aware of his presence. The next thing he knew, they were moving Larry's body from the back seat.

"This one is dead as well. The chauffeur is still alive."

By process of elimination, Nick realized that he was the other "dead one" in the car!

Panic began to set in as Nick noticed that he was unseen by those around him. As they removed Larry's body, he exited the car. He stood looking around at the accident scene. He noticed another ambulance with a gurney and a bagged body. He walked over to the body and unzipped the casing. He gasped when he viewed his own bloody face staring up at him.

"I know I'm dreaming. This isn't real."

Nick found his cell phone and dialed his office. Instead of his secretary's voice, he heard a voice that seemed familiar to him.

"Hello, Nicky. It's good to hear from you. I'll be there for you shortly. Entertain yourself for a little while."

The phone went dead.

Nick walked about the scene trying to get the attention of people. It was as though he didn't exist. His body was like a shadow that could pass through objects and people. Only his mind seemed intact. Terror was beginning to fill his entire being.

"Larry, if you're dead, where are you? Get over here, now."

He kept calling out Larry's name, but there was no response.

"Where the hell is that guy when you need him?"

Distracted by the number of police officers who were near his body, Nicky walked over to listen to their conversation.

"Well, the world is a safer place now that it is rid of the likes of him. We got Larry Klein's statement before he died. He wanted us to tell his wife and kids that he loved them. Then he stated that Nick Troiano was a murderer and thief. He told us he had the names, dates and events that the police needed to round up the worst scum in New York City. He expressed sorrow for his involvement with the Mob, and he then died."

"Damn that man. I always knew he didn't have the stomach for this business. Ah, go to hell, Larry!"

As Nick uttered these words, he turned to see an elegantly dressed man standing beside him.

"How's it going, Nicky?"

CHAPTER 29
PAT MARINO AND ANGELA

"Hear my prayer, O Lord, and give ear to my cry; hold not thy peace at my tears! For I am thy passing guest, a sojourner, like all my fathers. Look away from me, that I may know gladness, before I depart and be no more!"
(Psalm 39:12–13)

Pat's desperation knew no bounds. She wanted to be released from the torments she experienced in this place called hell. The stench of dead bodies, the filth of decaying flesh filled her nostrils and left her continually nauseated.

She found herself locked in what appeared to be a morgue. Steel drawers lined the wall. She assumed that dead bodies were inside them. She didn't dare ask herself what all this meant. All she knew was that she wanted out. She desperately wanted another chance.

Satan entered the morgue.

"Pretty nasty in here, isn't it, Pat?"

Pat looked at Satan and said nothing.

"Want to know what's behind drawer number one or drawer number two or drawer number three?"

Satan's questions met silence.

"Ah, play the game, Pat. You like to play games. Remember the Ouiji Board game?"

"I don't want to play games."

"Very well, let's just skip to drawer number four."

Pat found herself lying down in the drawer as it began to close into the wall. Unable to lift herself, as though someone or something were holding her down, she began screaming. She could hear Satan laughing as the drawer closed. She found herself in complete darkness. Lifting her hands above her, she felt only the top of the drawer. Kicking and thrashing from side to side, she realized she was trapped and helpless. She was entombed with no way out.

"How does it feel to be entombed, my little pet? Imagine being in the darkness of this coffin for all eternity, all alone without any hope of escape."

Then there was silence. Pat was filled with terror and desperation.

After several hours of struggling, Pat was exhausted. One thought filled her mind. "Please forgive me, Lord."

Suddenly, the drawer opened slowly. A young child stood several feet away. She was about 3 years old. Pat's eyes had to adjust to the light. Shaking violently, she crawled out of her metal tomb.

"Who are you, little girl? What are you doing here?"

"My name is Angela," she giggled. "That's because the angels named me."

Angela had short red curly hair. Her eyes were dark green.

"But, who are you?"

"I'm your daughter!"

Pat began to sob.

"But I destroyed you! Are you here to torment me, too?"

"Oh, Mommy, your guardian angel sent me to you to help you get out of this awful place."

"My guardian angel? Do I really have one?"

"Everyone has a guardian angel."

"Aren't you angry at me?"

She hesitated to use the word abortion because, after all, this was a child.

"When you aborted me, my guardian angel gathered me up and carried me to Jesus. He placed me right in Jesus' arms. Then Jesus smiled at me and kissed me. He told me I had a special place in his kingdom. He whispered to me that I had a special calling. I was to help you find your way home again."

"Did you suffer?"

"I don't suffer now. I have so many friends in heaven, and a beautiful mother who showers me with love. But she always reminds me that you are my mother as well, and that you need to find your way back to Jesus."

"Angela, I'm so sorry for what I did to you. Would you really help me find my way back?"

"Are you really sorry for all the bad things you did in your life?"

"Yes, Angela, I am sorry beyond words. But can you forgive me?"

"I forgave you the very moment I saw Jesus and he smiled at me. I know that you've thought about me. One night, you had a dream. Do you remember? In the dream, you wondered about me, where I was and what I would have looked like."

"Yes, I remember that dream. It was the first year after . . ."

"After you aborted me. Well, I have your dark green eyes!"

"And you have your father's red curly hair."

"I'll have to help him out, too. He never thinks about me. One day, when he gets married and has children, he will remember me. He will dream about me. I'll make sure of that!"

"May I touch you, Angela?"

"Give me your hand, Mommy. You need to follow me out of here to a safer place. Satan will be returning for you. He wants you very badly. He'll be back."

Pat took hold of her daughter's hand as tears rolled down her cheeks.

"Mommy, close your eyes for a second. I have a gift for you."

As Pat closed her eyes, she saw Angela transformed into an older child then an adolescent and then as she would have appeared as an adult. Then she saw hundreds of people. They all appeared, male and female, in beige robes.

"Angela, who are all those people I see?"

"They would have been your descendants through me."

Deep remorse filled Pat's heart as she realized that generations of people would not come into the world because of her choice.

"Do you see why abortion is so evil? You denied to God what he willed. Mommy, you see that man with the red hair and blue eyes at the end of the first row? He would have been your great-great-great grandson. He would have found a vaccine to destroy most types of cancer."

Pat couldn't bear to look any more.

"I'm so sorry! I am so terribly sorry. If they were never born, where are they?"

Angela touched her mother's cheek.

"They are in the mind and heart of God."

"I don't understand, Angela."

"I know. Just remember that God's mind and heart are eternal."

"There's so much I must atone for . . ."

CHAPTER 30
DENISE SMITH

Have mercy on me, O God, according to thy steadfast love; according to thy abundant mercy blot out my transgressions. Wash me thoroughly from my iniquity, and cleanse me from my sin! For I know my transgressions, and my sin is ever before me. Against thee, thee only, have I sinned, and done that which is evil in thy sight, so that thou art justified in thy sentence and blameless in thy judgment. Behold, I was brought forth in iniquity, and in sin did my mother conceive me.

(Psalm 51:1–5)

Denise felt empowered again to defend herself against the enemy after her meeting with Father Kassebart. Her confession lifted a tremendous burden from her shoulders.

Denise recalled the words of absolution, "And I absolve you from your sins, in the name of the Father, and of the Son, and of the Holy Spirit."

Then Father Kassebart warned her, "Denise, you are forgiven, but remember that Satan is trying to hunt you down to destroy you. Be vigilant. As the Scripture says, 'He is like a prowling lion looking for someone to devour. Resist him, solid in our faith.'"

She had asked Father Kassebart to open the door so she could escape.

"Only you can open that door."

Denise ran to the front door of the clinic.

"Only I can open the door?"

Satan reappeared by the reception desk.

"So, where do you think you're going, my little plum? Just because that priest stopped by doesn't mean a thing. I hate all those meddling priests. Wait till you see the bunch I have down here with me. Some of them were sexual predators of all flavors, some were heretics and some were thieves. The list goes on and on. I also have an attractive collection of bishops and cardinals down here! Great talkers they were. They loved consensus building, although there's not much of that down here! Anyway, I'll introduce all of them to you in good time. And, of course, they are my crowning glory! Now that fraud, Father Kassebart, is one of my greatest imposters!"

Denise knew that Satan was lying about Father Kassebart. During her confession, he helped her understand the gravity of her sins, especially the ones against chastity. He reminded her that her body was indeed a temple of God's Holy Spirit and that sins of the flesh desecrated that temple. He also told her that as embodied spirits, what we did in the body had consequences in eternity.

"You can't use your body to commit serious sins and expect God to reward you with eternal life. You must sincerely repent of all those sins you've committed in order to receive forgiveness," he cautioned Denise.

"What are you thinking, Denise?"

Realizing that Satan could no longer read her thoughts, she said aloud, "Praised be my Lord and Savior, Jesus Christ, now and for ages unending!"

Satan reeled almost in agony.

"You'll pay for this, you slut! Don't think you can escape. You'll weaken. You always do. Remember, I know you, Denise. I know all your sins!"

With those words, he vanished.

Denise walked over to the door again. She attempted to turn the knob, but it still didn't budge. Leaning up against the door, she closed her eyes.

"What did he mean, only I can open the door?"

Turning to face the door again, she shrieked in horror because it was gone.

CHAPTER 31
JACKSON ROKER AND GRANDMA PEARL

Behold, thou desirest truth in the inward being; therefore teach me wisdom in my secret heart.

(Psalm 51:6)

Grandma Pearl gestured to Jay to kiss her on the cheek.

"I've got to go now, Jay. You do everything I told you to do the next time that old devil shows up. Remember, he's really a coward, has nothing of any real value to say and generally lies through his teeth. Don't listen to him. Don't pay him any mind."

"He scares me!"

"You have only one thing to be scared of, Jay. Be scared of losing your soul! He can't do anything to you unless you surrender to him. He wants you to sin. Now show me what I taught you!"

Jay took his right hand and put it to his forehead, then to the middle of his chest, and then to his left shoulder and right shoulder.

"Father, Son and Holy Spirit, protect me," Jay whispered.

"That's right. That devil can't stand when you invoke God. Say that prayer with faith!"

"Grandma Pearl, what is heaven like?"

"It's beyond anything you can ask for, imagine or desire! But right now, you get yourself ready to face that devil like I taught you."

Jay kissed his grandmother.

"If you see I need help, please come back, Grandma."

She smiled and vanished from his sight.

Satan appeared again and strolled toward Jay.

"Did that disgusting woman leave? When she was on Earth, she gave me grief. Now that she's in the other place, she's a constant annoyance. Always praying for people and interceding for them. You know, most people are afraid of me, but your grandmother feared no one, not even me! She would have been a great catch. And Jackson, I know what she's trying to do for you. But she won't succeed. You know why? Because you're lost forever! She can pray all she wants, but you're mine."

Jay felt empowered by his Grandma Pearl's visit.

Turning to Satan, he made the sign of the cross and said, "Depart from me, you evil spirit."

Satan laughed heartily.

Mocking Jay's words, he repeated, "Depart from me, you evil spirit! Why, your Grandma Pearl used to say that each time I tried to suggest something naughty to her. Only with her, it worked!"

Taking Jay by the throat, he lifted him from the ground.

"I am your Lord and Master. Where's Grandma Pearl now, Jackson?"

Jay felt his airway constricted. He tried to pry Satan's hands from his neck.

Feeling the intense pain of being choked and unable to help himself, he cried out in his mind, "I offer this prayer up for a woman contemplating abortion at this moment."

Satan immediately released his grip and gasped.

"Playing games with me, are you?"

Grabbing Jay by the shoulder, Satan forced him back into the elevator.

"Come on, hero. I'll show you who's the boss."

CHAPTER 32
SHELLEY DeSIMONE

Cast me not away from thy presence, and take not thy holy Spirit from me. Restore to me the joy of thy salvation, and uphold me with a willing spirit. Then I will teach transgressors thy ways, and sinners will return to thee.
(Psalm 51:11–13)

Shelley could no longer smell her mother's familiar perfume or visualize her parents standing at the foot of her bed. The warmth that she felt in their presence was gone. It was replaced by a piercing cold. Unable to move and open her eyes, she felt a cold hand touch her arm.

"Shelley, I've come for you. You wanted to end your life, and I couldn't bear to lose you! Open your eyes."

Shelley opened her eyes. It was Mark. At first, she was delighted to see him, but then she remembered her conversation with her parents.

"You were never mine," Shelley said aloud.

She sat up in her bed and looked around the room. The glass was still on her night table and the bottle of pills was empty.

"How is it that I woke up?"

"Let's not talk about that right now. I'm here for you. I never want to be separated from you."

Mark reached over to embrace Shelley.

"No, Mark. Don't."

"Aren't you glad to see me? You did this to yourself because of me. Please don't reject me."

Shelley rose from her bed.

"Where is the ambulance? They have to take me to the hospital and pump my stomach."

"Shelley, I love you. Come to me."

"Get away from me!"

The cold in the room was intense by this time. Shelley was shivering. The man who appeared to be Mark moved around the bed toward her. Shelley instinctively recoiled from him.

"You're not Mark."

Shelley made the sign of the cross. She glanced at the man standing before her. It was no longer Mark, but a handsome man in a navy blue suit.

"Shelley, you're right. I'm not Mark. I'm better than Mark. I am for you."

As Shelley was about to respond, she could hear within her soul the words, "Resist him, Michelle."

"I am sorry for my sins!"

Shelley did not speak aloud, but in her heart. She named her sins. As she did this, the man in the navy blue suit stepped further away from her. Tears filled her eyes. She walked over to her dresser and opened the top drawer. She rummaged in it for the crucifix that her parents had given to her as a teenager. She had removed this sign of her faith when she stopped going to Mass. She lifted the crucifix and kissed it then placed it around her neck.

"Forgive me, Lord."

Satan was no longer visible. Within seconds, she found herself back in her bed, unable to open her eyes or move. She could hear a bell ringing in the background, but she couldn't identify it.

CHAPTER 33
DR. SAMUEL WEISS AND ETHEL WEISS

For thou hast no delight in sacrifice; were I to give a burnt offering, thou wouldst not be pleased. The sacrifice acceptable to God is a broken spirit; a broken and contrite heart, O God, thou wilt not despise. Do good to Zion in thy good pleasure; rebuild the walls of Jerusalem, then wilt thou delight in right sacrifices, in burnt offerings and whole burnt offerings; then bulls will be offered on thy altar.

(Psalm 51:16–19)

Sam sat at his desk knowing full well that he would be paid a visit. Satan strolled in with an air of arrogance.

"Well, Dr. Weiss, how does it feel to be in hell? I know you wanted to retire to Florida, but the flames of hell will keep you warm in the winter!"

Satan was amused with himself.

"Actually, it can get rather cold down here. I hear you had a visit from your daughter, Helene. What a shame that you'll never see her again. Did she tell you that retard, Bernie, sent her?"

Sam said nothing.

"Cat got your tongue, Sammy? Aside from those pesky little demons down here, I'll be your only visitor for all of eternity. You might as well try to be a little more congenial."

Sam took a blank sheet of paper from his desk. He dated it and addressed it to his daughter, Helene.

December 7
Dear Helene,

When you died so violently 24 years ago, I was filled with hatred and bitterness. I was angry at God for taking you from me. I lost what little faith I had. Life became meaningless to me.

A year after your death, I opened the Caring Clinic for Women. Why bring children into the world when death was so inevitable and so brutal a reality? Money and pleasure are soothing balms for a lost soul. I was a lost soul.

Several years into the business, I even contemplated suicide. I felt like a coward when I couldn't inject myself with the overdose of morphine. Something inside of me cried for life. But, despite my own desire to live, I found myself locked into taking the lives of others. I have been responsible for taking approximately 4,000 lives a year in my abortion business. That's 4,000 babies killed a year for the last 13 years. May God have mercy on my eternal soul!

When you appeared to me, you told me that Satan used me to destroy all those children who belonged to God. I can never bring those babies back to life, but I rejoice that the Lord of life has rescued them from the pit of nothingness. They now live in his eternal presence. Only such a Provident God can bring good out of the tremendous evil I inflicted upon them and their mothers.

My dearest child, my Helene, I find myself locked in this awesome struggle to save my soul. You assured me that it is God who will save my soul, if I only permit him to do so.

I entrust my soul to God, and I desire with all my being to dwell in the heavenly castle that awaits me. You told me that in our Father's house there are many dwelling places and that one is being prepared for me. May I find myself in that dwelling place that has been prepared for me for all eternity.

I long for forgiveness of all my sins. I long for everlasting peace. Most of all, I long for eternal love and for the joy of being in the presence of the great "I AM."

Intuitively, I know that this Jesus, whom Satan hates, is the one who will rescue me from death and damnation. I wish to cling to him for all eternity. May he lead me to the place where the patriarchs, prophets and saints dwell in light.

I conclude this letter with a cry to heaven for mercy. I will attempt, before my death, to do something to reverse some of the evil that I have unleashed in the world through the Caring Clinic for Women.

Samuel Weiss,
the greatest of sinners

Rage was written all over Satan's face as the contents of the letter became clear to him. Reaching over to destroy the letter, he hissed as it easily eluded his grasp then floated away and disappeared from sight.

Sam turned toward Satan.

"My daughter is taking that letter to heaven."

"You'll never escape me, Sam. No one escapes me!"

Sam stood up. He faced Satan and said, "My body is presently lying in a pool of blood in my garage. A thief entered the garage and knocked me unconscious as I was about to turn the alarm off. I am dying, but not yet dead. God has allowed me this one last opportunity to repent of my sins. Just as I signed a contract to destroy unborn children, I now formally submit, in writing, my confession of sin and request for mercy and forgiveness."

Enraged, Satan screamed, "You don't know what you are talking about. You are dead and damned! There is no mercy for you."

"Yes, you certainly are the father of lies. You twist the truth and engage in every type of deceit. For the first time in my life, I see things clearly, rightly, justly. I see the truth. I see all my many sins as clearly as I see you. More importantly, I feel great sorrow at having offended God. I am again a man of faith. I choose to hope in God's mercy and I desire to die a man of love. I even forgive the thief who is responsible for my death. As for you, I reject you, you wretched creature. I fully and without reserve abandon myself to the Almighty . . ."

Suddenly, Sam found himself back in his garage. He was lying face up as medics worked on him. Blood was oozing from the back of his head.

"Dr. Weiss. Dr. Weiss, can you hear us?"

"Oh, Sammy, it's Ethel. Oh, my Sammy!"

Ethel had been in the house the whole time he was in the garage. She had heard her husband park the car, but when he didn't come into the house she ventured into the garage and found him on the floor in a pool of his own blood. The thief had taken his wallet then panicked and ran when he heard Ethel scream.

"Ethel, listen to me carefully. Sell the abortion clinic. All the money must go to charity. The bank accounts must all go to charity. Keep only the money that I earned honestly. Do you hear me? I've seen Helene."

His voice trailed off.

"Oh, dear God," cried Ethel.

"What's the matter, Mrs. Weiss?" asked the medic.

She remained silent.

"Ethel, come close and listen. I'm not hallucinating. Do as I tell you. There is a God and an afterlife. You must do this for me and for us. Do you understand? Get rid of the abortion clinic. Donate the property to a worthy cause."

"Oh, Sammy, don't leave me, please."

"Do you understand? I have to make good on a promise."

Ethel whispered into her husband's ear, "I understand. You should never have opened that damn clinic."

Relief was evident on Sam's face.

"You were always right. I love you, Ethel."

His eyes looked away from her.

"He's gone, Mrs. Weiss."

Ethel noticed the serene smile on her dead husband's face.

Sam's eyes were still open. They were gazing up. In death, Sam's eyes were focused on his daughter.

"Daddy, I'm here. I've come for you."

Sam lifted himself out of his body without effort. Before he stood up, he bent over and kissed his wife on the cheek. Ethel touched her cheek as tears streamed down her face.

"Mrs. Weiss, we found these things in your husband's hand."

The medic placed a child's charm bracelet and a blue rabbit's foot in her hands.

Ethel grasped the bracelet then brought it to her lips and kissed it.

"This was my daughter's bracelet."

Without saying more, she said to herself in silence, " . . . We buried her with it."

Ethel took the rabbit's foot in her hand. It was attached to a key chain. The name BERNIE WEISS and a telephone number were written on it.

"Oh, God, this was his brother's keychain. He carried it with him everywhere he went as a child."

"Where have you been, my dear husband? You did see Helene."

Ethel vowed to respect her husband's last wishes.

"Rest in peace, my love."

Ethel kissed her husband goodbye. The medics helped her to her feet, then she fainted in their arms.

Sam turned around to look back at his wife. He really did love her. He wanted her to be with him someday. It disturbed him to see her faint.

"Daddy, it's time. Mom will be all right. She's a strong woman. Look at the light. Everyone is waiting for you with great joy!"

Sam hesitated, but then felt drawn to follow the light. Helene and Sam walked away from Westchester and found themselves on a wooded path.

"Where are we, Helene?"

"We're crossing over. See the light ahead?"

The light became more and more brilliant as they continued walking. Colorful flowers, trees of all kinds and shrubbery lined the path.

"I'm so unworthy, Helene. I've done so much evil. The light is so strong! It's blinding me!"

"Daddy, don't be afraid. Take my hand. I'll lead you. The light will heal you."

Sam cried tears of sorrow for his many sins then experienced great joy in discovering that God filled his being.

"Daddy, keep walking with me toward the light. You need to complete this part of the journey with me. The Lamb of God awaits you."

Sam continued walking. The light became like a burning bush that was unconsumed.

"I am so unworthy."

Helene let go of her father's hand. She reached up to kiss him.

"Now you need to finish the journey on your own," she said, and then disappeared.

Sam's angel indicated to him that he should remove his shoes. Sam did so and dropped to his knees. He hid his face in his hands in the presence of the great "I AM." Love flooded his soul. He knew the ultimate encounter with God was about to take place, and he began to see as he had never seen before.

CHAPTER 34
JAY ROKER AND GRANDMA PEARL

Be merciful to me, O God, be merciful to me, for in thee my soul takes refuge; in the shadow of thy wings I will take refuge, till the storms of destruction pass by. I cry to God Most High, to God who fulfills his purpose for me. He will send from heaven and save me, he will put to shame those who trample upon me. God will send forth his steadfast love and his faithfulness!

(Psalm 57:1–3)

Jay found himself standing by the black abyss listening to the cries from tortured souls below him. He remembered his instructions from Grandma Pearl.

"There is hope for me."

Satan appeared again.

"Jay, I think it's time for you to meet some of your friends down there. They're a hateful bunch, you know. The great thing about hell is that just when you think you can't take much more pain and agony, there's a lot more to experience!"

Jay lifted his mind and heart to Jesus.

"Even if I should walk through the valley of death, I shall fear no evil," he said, quoting a passage from Psalm 23.

Satan look startled. Jay continued to pray silently.

"Whatever I suffer, I offer back to you, dear Savior, for the salvation of souls. First, I want to offer up my sufferings for the women contemplating abortions at the Caring Clinic for Women. I offer my suffering for all those women who now grieve because of their abortions. I pray for the conversion of hearts. In particular, I pray for the soul of Dr. Samuel Weiss. May he find forgiveness, healing and peace."

Turning away from Satan, Jay said, "Into your hands, Jesus, I commend my body and spirit. Forgive my sins, and I will never presume on your mercy and love again. Rescue me from the likes of this evil creature and spare my soul."

Jay found himself sprawled on the snow-covered street in Jackson Heights, Queens, where he was being taken care of by paramedics. He never did make it into Marty's store. A speeding car struck him as he exited his car without looking for oncoming traffic.

The medic had applied something to his chest. His heart had stopped, but they were able to shock it back into a normal rhythm.

"His pulse is back. I think he's conscious."

The pain was excruciating in his left leg and left arm. His chest felt as though someone had tossed a refrigerator on top of him.

Jay thought, "I offer this all up for the salvation of souls."

He heard the medic say, "I think he may lose that leg. He's losing too much blood. Let's get him to the hospital."

Jay knew that he was going to die, but not quite yet. His Grandma Pearl told him that he would suffer much before he entered God's kingdom.

"Are you strong enough to suffer out of love? Can you follow the example of Jesus?" she asked him.

Jay said he would willingly offer his last agonizing moments in the body, and his last labored breath on earth in an act of love.

As the medics moved Jay, each movement intensified the agony he felt in his body.

"Jay, we know you are in a lot of pain right now. Just bear with it a little longer. We're not far from the hospital."

Jay turned his mind to Pat Marino, Dr. Weiss, the clinic workers and the girls who were scheduled for abortions.

"I offer all this for you . . ." Jay thought before he lost consciousness.

When he opened his eyes again, he saw his Grandma Pearl sitting next to the medic who was working to keep him alive.

"Well, Jackson, it won't be long before you cross over. Keep praying."

"Can I really help them?"

"You sure can! Offer your final moments for their conversions!"

"You're a smart woman, Granny Pearl!"

"It's almost time, Jackson. Prepare yourself to meet the King of Kings and Lord of Lords! Start letting go now. You are crossing over . . ."

"We're losing him. Gosh, I thought we had a chance to save him," the young medic exclaimed.

Grandma Pearl laughed.

"Oh, but he is being saved!"

"I'm scared, Granny."

"Now, Jackson. Be brave. I'm here to help you."

"He's gone," the medic said. "What time do you have for the record?"

As the medics began to enter the information about Jay's death on their medical forms, they noted that their patient had died with a smile on his face.

"Well, get moving Jackson."

Jay lifted himself out of his body. Together, he and his grandmother walked through the door of the ambulance.

The street was transformed before their eyes. A beautiful white marble stairway leading into the clouds appeared before them.

"See that stairway? Let's climb the mountain of the Lord, Jay."

Then Grandma Pearl began humming an old Negro spiritual she had learned as a child. Jay took his grandmother's hand and they began walking toward a brilliant light.

"Grandma Pearl, there's Dr. Weiss. He's walking toward the light! I don't understand . . ."

"You'll understand everything in a few minutes. Look, Jay, there's Mary. She's smiling at you!"

"She's so beautiful!"

Mary was wearing a white gown with a blue sash around her waist. Her arms were extended toward Jay. A brilliant light surrounded her image.

Suddenly, Jay stopped. The pain he felt earlier in his body could not equal the pain he was experiencing now as he realized the evil of his sins and how they had offended Jesus.

"That's how it is, Jay. The closer you get to God, the more you suffer when you think how you offended him. Mary will lead you to the Lord. "

Jay felt intense joy, a joy that was beyond words.

Grandma Pearl let go of Jay's hand.

"You go on now. Go to your mother. She'll take you to Jesus. My work is done. Grandma Pearl will see you real soon. Go ahead, boy. Follow her."

Jay kissed his grandmother and confidently walked toward the woman in white. She gestured for him to follow her to the light.

CHAPTER 35
PAT MARINO

*Save me, O God! For the waters have come up to my neck.
I sink in deep mire, where there is no foothold; I have
come into deep waters, and the flood sweeps over me. I
am weary with my crying; my throat is parched. My eyes
grow dim with waiting for my God.*

(Psalm 69:1–3)

Angela disappeared from the morgue. Pat stood in the middle of the room waiting for the inevitable.

"Well, Patricia, you've met the child you destroyed. Sweet kid. That doesn't change anything! She was innocent of your crime, but you are guilty as sin!"

Thinking himself so clever, Satan added, "Anyway, that was all a figment of your imagination!"

For a split second, Pat doubted what she had seen. But then she remembered all the things that Angela told her to do in order to elude Satan's grasp.

"What are you thinking, my little pet?"

"I'm thinking that I was sinful as a teenager and that I invited you into my soul. The games with the occult, the irreligious acts we committed, the sins against the Commandments, these were all serious sins."

"Good, now that we understand each other . . ."

"No, we don't understand each other. You are evil incarnate. Evil is not to be understood, it must simply be rejected. I don't want anything to do with you."

"But you just told me that you are a sinner! You admit your guilt! This is the place where people go when they are guilty! Don't you get it, you fool?"

"I am a sinner in need of forgiveness. I wish to repent."

"You can't do that in hell. I told you that already."

"Angela told me that I slipped on my afghan in the apartment as I tried to answer the door. Mrs. Fitzpatrick ran into her apartment to get the key I had given her to my apartment. She found me unconscious on the floor and called the police. Medics are treating me as we speak. The Lord is giving me a second chance."

"That old biddy, Mrs. Fitzpatrick, is always meddling in people's lives. Too bad she took such a sickening interest in you!"

"Yes, she did take an interest in me. What I didn't know was that she prayed for me daily. She never preached to me about the evil of abortion. She knew I would close her out of my life. Instead, she prayed for me in silence. Angela told me she even offered up her arthritic pains for me. Imagine an elderly woman offering her pain for a sinner like me! All she ever told me was that she praying for me to find a decent job with security and to meet a nice man who would treat me with respect and love."

"Those old ladies can really be a pain. You know her days are numbered. Did Angela tell you Mrs. Fitzpatrick is dying?"

"Yes, but she won't be making any pit stops here to see the likes of you!"

"I'm touched, Pat. Truly I am. But hell will be all the more cruel since you can't go back now."

"I am going back. You have no power over me. And now, with my whole heart and soul, I renew my Catholic faith and turn to Christ and his Church. I make a special appeal to St. Michael the Archangel to rescue me from the likes of you."

"St. Michael! He was always a bit pushy."

"Silence. I surrender myself to the Lord of life and entrust my salvation to him."

St. Michael the Archangel appeared and Satan recoiled into a corner. With a look of disdain on his face, the archangel raised his shield.

"Pat, take hold of my shield."

As she reached with both hands to clutch St. Michael's shield, she felt as though a whirlwind had encircled her and was transporting her away from the dreadful place she knew as hell. In an instant, she found herself in her apartment, sprawled on the floor.

"She's coming around. That was a mighty nasty fall you had, young lady," said the paramedic. "We'll take you to the hospital to get an X-ray or two of your head. Did you know you have a fever of 103 degrees?"

The medic didn't share with Pat that at one point they couldn't feel her pulse. There was no point worrying her about something they couldn't explain. Her pulse was strong enough now.

Pat looked around and saw Mrs. Fitzpatrick standing with her daughter, Beverly, near the door.

"Mrs. Fitz!"

"I knew something was wrong when you didn't open the door. I heard you at the door then there was dead silence. I ran into my apartment to get the key. Beverly and I discovered you lying on the floor behind the door wrapped in that afghan. May I buy you an electric blanket for Christmas, dear? I think it's safer."

"Oh, Mrs. Fitz. Thank you for all your prayers and sacrifices on my behalf."

Mrs. Fitzpatrick looked at Pat, puzzled by her comment.

"My daughter, Beverly, will drive us to the hospital. She's in the kitchen turning off the kettle. It's been whistling for the last five minutes! She'll call your parents on her cell phone."

"O.K. Let's get her downstairs into the ambulance," the medic said.

As Pat was being carried to the ambulance, she spotted a little girl about 3 years old standing on the sidewalk. She had curly red hair and dark green eyes.

"Angela!"

The little girl put her index finger over her lips.

"Ssshh." Then she winked at Pat.

Pat leaned back on the stretcher as the doors to the ambulance were closed. She was laughing.

The medic looked concerned.

"Are you O.K.?"

"I'm fine. That little girl reminded me of someone I was talking to a while ago."

The two paramedics looked at each other with raised eyebrows. Neither man had seen a little girl, and a little while ago Pat had been unconscious. One of the paramedics remarked, "It must be the high fever."

Pat closed her eyes and pictured Angela. She felt warm for the first time in a long time.

CHAPTER 36
DENISE SMITH AND JOSHUA SMITH

Blessed be the Lord, who daily bears us up; God is our salvation. Our God is a God of salvation; and to God, the Lord, belongs escape from death.

(Psalm 68:19–20)

Denise was horrified to learn that the door had disappeared.

"How am I going to open a door that doesn't exist?"

She could hear Satan laughing, though she didn't see him.

"Go ahead, Denise. Open the door!" he said sarcastically.

Out of the corner of her eye, Denise saw a little boy. He was about 6 years old, and had blond hair with bangs and steel-blue eyes. There was something familiar about him.

"Who are you?"

"My name is Joshua."

"Joshua? Do I know you?"

"Denise, I am the little boy your mother miscarried. I am your brother! I am coming to you as a child, the age you were when I died."

Denise smiled.

"You certainly look like a Smith! Are you in heaven, too?"

"Yes."

"Joshua, how can I open a door that doesn't exist?"

"You have to open the door of your heart. Take my hand and close your eyes. Do you still see me?"

"Yes, I see you."

Denise took her brother's hand and began to walk with him. After passing through the front door as though it were only a shadow, she found herself outside the clinic. She couldn't see clearly where they were going. A fog enveloped them.

"The door you must open leads to life. Look ahead."

Denise saw the steps leading to All Saints Church.

"My spiritual life began through those front doors," she reflected. "I was baptized in this church."

Joshua smiled and disappeared.

"I'll see you again when it is your time to cross over."

Denise began to climb the steps to her parish church. She gazed at the wooden doors, and then reached for the ornate handle. She could hear Satan screaming obscenities behind her as she turned the handle . . .

"Denise, wake up, honey. Your father and I want to talk to you."

Denise realized that she was in her own room and in her own bed. The stuffed bear was still in her arms. Confused and dazed, she glanced at her wristwatch. It was five-thirty on Friday night, December 7.

"Come in. I'm awake now. Mom and Dad, you won't believe the nightmare I just had! I need to talk to the two of you."

"Before you say anything, we have some terrible news. Brenda's mother just called. Brenda has been in a terrible car accident. Apparently, a man got out of his car without looking for oncoming traffic. He was struck by a car and died earlier today. Brenda was behind the vehicle that struck the man they identified as a security guard. A truck plowed into her car, unable to stop in time. Her car looks like a crushed orange juice can. It's a miracle she is still alive. They don't know for sure if she is going to make it."

Denise's father looked intently at his daughter.

"Brenda has been calling for you. She is conscious. She keeps saying, 'Denise, don't do it!' "

"I need to see Brenda tonight!"

Maggie Smith looked with concern at her daughter.

"Let's all go together. Denise, maybe the most important lesson for all of us tonight is that life is a precious gift from God, not to be taken for granted."

Denise turned to both her parents and added, "It's a gift of infinite value."

CHAPTER 37
SHELLEY DeSIMONE

He only is my rock and my salvation, my fortress; I shall not be shaken. On God rests my deliverance and my honor; my mighty rock, my refuge is God. Trust in him at all times, O people; pour out your heart before him; God is a refuge for us.

(Psalm 62:6–8)

As Shelley opened her eyes, she realized she was in a hospital. A doctor and a nurse were standing beside her.

"You are one lucky young woman. Your neighbors were concerned about you and entered your apartment, where they found you unconscious in your bedroom. You had left your keys in the front door. What made you do it?"

"I was a fool."

The sound in the background that Shelley heard was not a bell, but rather the beep of a machine monitoring her heart rate.

"You will pull through, but I must stress that you were very lucky this time. Your neighbor, who is a retired pharmacist, was able to tell the medics exactly what pills you took. Dr. John Andersen, a psychiatrist on staff, will be in to visit you shortly. Is there anyone we should call?"

"I'd like to speak to the chaplain, a Catholic priest."

"We'll arrange for a chaplain to visit."

Shelley felt humiliated. She had attempted suicide and now everyone thought she was crazy. Maybe she had lost her mind momentarily, but she had regained her sanity through the grace of God.

"How can I tell a shrink what really happened? I definitely can't tell him that I spoke to my dead parents and Satan, who was disguised as Mark. He'll lock me up and throw away the key!"

As Shelley considered how to make sense out of her experience, a Catholic priest walked into her hospital room. The elderly priest stood beside her hospital bed.

"Hello. My name is Father Thaddeus Brown."

"I'm glad you were not successful in taking your own life! I've been praying for you since they brought you into the emergency room. Tell me, what happened that you did this to yourself?"

Shelley shared her story with this gentle soul, who listened with great patience. As a Catholic who had fallen away from the practice of her faith, she readily admitted her sins to the priest, and was consoled to hear the words of absolution that the priest read from his ritual book. He then encouraged her to be courageous as she faced the consequences of her actions.

Nothing frightened her, not even the probing questions that Dr. Andersen would ask her or the opinions her neighbors might have regarding her mental stability. She knew that she had regained her sanity and discovered the value of her life before God.

Shelley decided that would tell the psychiatrist that God turned her unsuccessful suicide attempt into a personal triumph for her. She smiled as she realized that God had given her a second chance at life.

As Dr. Andersen entered the room, Father Brown excused himself. As he left, he gave Shelly a thumbs-up sign.

"I'll check on you later."

Shelley smiled at Dr. Andersen and extended her hand to shake his hand.

"It's a pleasure to meet you, Dr. Andersen. I was expecting you."

Dr. Andersen was disarmed.

"The pleasure is mine," he said.

CHAPTER 38
DENISE SMITH
AND BRENDA HERMANN

Hear my cry, O God, listen to my prayer; from the end of the earth I call to thee, when my heart is faint. Lead thou me to the rock that is higher than I; for thou art my refuge, a strong tower against the enemy. Let me dwell in thy tent for ever! Oh to be safe under the shelter of thy wings!
(Psalm 61:1–4)

    Denise and her parents waited for Brenda's parents, Kay and George Hermann, to emerge from the Intensive Care Unit.

    Kay turned to Maggie and said, "This is a nightmare. We'll know more in 24 hours."

    Tears began to stream down Kay's face as her husband put his arms around her.

    "Well, we'll just have to pray real hard for your daughter," Maggie whispered gently. She took out her rosary and placed it in Kay's hand.

    "Why don't we all sit down?" said John as he gestured toward the waiting area.

    "Oh, Denise, go see Brenda," Kay said. "She keeps asking for you, honey. Just tell the nurse who you are. They'll let you in."

    Denise walked through the automatic double doors into ICU. The nurse made the necessary inquiries. When the nurse learned that Denise was Brenda's best friend, she gestured for Denise to go over to her bed.

    "Brenda has been asking for you."

Pointing to the curtained area to her left, she indicated that Brenda was being cared for there.

"Don't stay too long. She's not a pretty sight, so prepare yourself."

Brenda walked slowly to her best friend's bed. Parting the curtains, she entered and stood before Brenda. Her beaten, bruised and swollen face was startling. Brenda's eyes were closed and her strawberry blond hair was in disarray around her face.

"Brenda. Brenda. It's Denise."

Brenda opened her bloodshot green eyes.

"Oh, Denise, please, you mustn't do it!"

In a low voice, Denise whispered, "Brenda, I am not having the abortion. Calm down."

"Denise, I've been somewhere where no one should ever go. It was so awful! I was terrified!"

"Brenda, I was there, too! That's why I am not having the abortion."

Brenda looked into Denise's eyes.

"Where were you?"

"Let's just say I had a hell of a nightmare!"

"Denise, I really experienced hell! I'm so afraid, and it's not over yet. Please, stay with me. I don't want to fall asleep! He's after me."

"Relax, Brenda. Everything is going to be O.K. I'll stay here and pray with you. When you pray with all your heart, he's powerless. We can talk later. Try to rest. Just close your eyes. You're safe now."

"No, I'm not safe . . ."

Denise slipped her hand into her pocket and took out her rosary.

"Brenda, I'm going to start praying the rosary."

Placing another rosary in her friend's hand, she made the sign of the cross. Then she took out a small plastic holy water container, put some of the water on her thumb and signed Brenda's forehead with the cross.

As Denise began to pray the rosary, Brenda started to relax and breathe more normally.

"Please, don't let me fall sleep . . . ," Brenda whispered.

However, within minutes, she was sound asleep.

Five minutes later, the nurse peeked in and looked at Brenda.

"Don't try to wake her. You can return again tomorrow. She seems more peaceful now. She was so agitated earlier."

Denise placed her rosary in her pocket. Quietly and prayerfully she exited ICU and looked for the hospital chapel to continue her prayers for her best friend.

CHAPTER 39
BRENDA HERMANN

Make me to know thy ways, O Lord; teach me thy paths. Lead me in thy truth, and teach me, for thou art the God of my salvation; for thee I wait all the day long. Be mindful of thy mercy, O Lord, and of thy steadfast love, for they have been from of old. Remember not the sins of my youth, or my transgressions; according to thy steadfast love remember me, for thy goodness' sake, O Lord!
(Psalm 25:4–7)

Brenda found herself face to face with Satan once more.

"So, you've been talking to your little friend, Denise. She's gotten awfully religious lately. Was that real holy water she doused you with?"

"I told her not to have the abortion."

"And you think that's going to release you from my control? Do you think that holy water or a rosary can keep you safe from me? You're not even Catholic, Brenda," Satan said sarcastically.

"No, but my best friend is! I love her and trust her. If she believes that the blessed water and the rosary have power then I believe it as well."

"How touching! Those things can't save you, my little pumpkin. You've made too many wrong choices in life."

"Yes, I was wrong about a lot of things. But now I understand the truth!"

"Next you'll tell me you oppose gay marriage!"

"I do."

"So, you want to judge your neighbor."

"No, I reject what is sinful."

"So, who has enlightened you about the moral life, my little pumpkin? Has some Catholic theologian been instructing you since our last tête-à-tête?"

"I thought you knew everything!" Brenda quipped.

Like Denise, Brenda had done her undergraduate work at St. Vincent's University. And like Denise, she took a Theology course with Monsignor Noone, who was now the vicar general of the diocese.

During these encounters with Satan, Brenda realized that in a split second, long conversations, events and experiences could be relived. She recalled one class that dealt with marriage. One of the female students, a hardcore feminist and an avowed member of the National Organization of Women, had argued in favor of civil unions and religious unions between same-sex partners. She had raised the objection that the Church had no right to condemn such unions.

"Jill, the Church teaches that marriage can only be properly understood as existing between a man and a woman. The Bible teaches that marriage began with the Lord's creation of the first man and woman. The two became one flesh. God gave marriage its definition.

"We may define a thing as we wish, but that doesn't change the reality of the thing. Remember our earlier discussions about truth and reality? For example, you may define the moon as that object in the sky around which all the planets revolve. You may attribute to it the properties of the sun, but it is not the sun and the planets do not revolve around it. Correct?"

"True, but this is different, Monsignor!"

Monsignor Noone continued, "Let me finish, Jill. A person may attempt to define marriage as a relationship between two men or two women, but this does not change the reality of how God defines marriage. Reality must be based on God's truth.

"Once you redefine marriage to include people of the same sex, there's no end to the redefinitions. Why can't marriage exist between a man and dog, a woman and a chimpanzee or two men, two women and three dogs! It goes on and on."

Satan distracted Brenda by pointing to her motionless body on the hospital bed.

"Your thoughts bore me, Brenda. Look, you are dying, my little pumpkin."

Brenda noticed the doctor and nurse standing over her body. They seemed concerned as they watched the monitors.

"I'm betting that you won't make it through the next 24 hours! Then we can continue our theological discussions ad nauseam!"

Before she could respond, Brenda found herself back in her hospital bed. The doctor and nurse had moved away from her bedside. She felt the rosary in her hand and held on to it tightly. She opened her eyes and looked for Denise.

"Denise told me to tell you she went into the chapel to continue praying the rosary," the nurse explained. "You know, a very handsome gentleman just came to the desk and was inquiring about your condition. I had to tell him that we don't give out information because of the HIPPA regulations."

"What handsome gentleman?"

"He was in his late twenties or early thirties and quite well-dressed. I believe his name was Eric Luf. At any rate, I told him to contact your family for information about your condition. Who is the handsome admirer?"

"What did he say?"

"Not much. Oh, yes. He said he can't wait to see you again!"

"Eric Luf . . . Eric Luf . . ."

Brenda thought about his name.

"What is it about that name?"

"Oh, yes. He referred to you as his 'little pump-kin.'"

Brenda suddenly realized that the name Eric Luf spelled LUCIFER when the letters were rearranged.

Brenda tightened her grip on the rosary.

"If he returns, keep him away from me. Do you hear me? Keep him away from me!"

The nurse straightened up, concerned that she had agitated Brenda.

"I thought he was a friend. I'll leave a message at the desk for the other nurses that he's not to disturb you."

"He's probably an ex-boyfriend," thought the nurse.

CHAPTER 40
MICHAEL REID AND
SISTER MARY GRACE DONNELLAN

Turn thou to me, and be gracious to me; for I am lonely and afflicted. Relieve the troubles of my heart, and bring me out of my distresses. Consider my affliction and my trouble, and forgive all my sins.

(Psalm 25:16–18)

Michael Reid pressed the play button on the tape recorder.

"Sister, how long have you been in religious life?"

Silence.

"Was religion an important part of your life?"

More silence.

"So you've always been a practicing Catholic?"

Still more silence.

"Beth, your grandniece, told me that you've been diagnosed with terminal cancer."

Silence.

"Yes, and please address that. And call me Michael."

More silence.

"What do you mean your 'recent death experience?' You talk about death as though it were an accomplished fact."

Michael pressed the stop button. He scratched his head.

"What the heck?"

"Turn the recorder off, Michael. Dial my convent number and ask for me."

Obediently, he read the number of her convent written on the folder and dialed it.

"Immaculate Heart Convent. May I help you?"

"Ah, yes, my name is Professor Michael Reid from Brooklyn College. I'd like to speak to Sister Mary Grace Donnellan."

With a little hesitation in her voice, the Sister responded, "Just a moment, sir. I'm switching you to Sister Mary Rose, our house coordinator."

"Sister Mary Rose. May I help you?"

"My name is Professor Michael Reid. I have an appointment tomorrow with Sister Mary Grace Donnellan. How is Sister feeling? Is she feeling well enough for the interview?"

"Professor, Sister Mary Grace passed on earlier this morning. She died a very peaceful death. We don't know how, but her wheelchair was left in her room and her body was discovered in our chapel. She was actually lying in her pew as if asleep. No one can figure out how she went from her room to the chapel unescorted!"

Michael could barely believe his ears.

"Please extend my condolences to your community and to her family."

Sister Mary Rose thanked him and gave him the viewing times and the information regarding her funeral Mass. He hung up the phone. Sister Mary Grace was no longer seated on the chair by his desk. He looked at the chair and noticed a handwritten note. He picked up the undated note and trembled as he read it.

Dear Michael,

You have many questions about life and death and the role of religion in human life. The real question is whether or not you choose to believe in God. You claim to be an atheist. I know you are not.

Let me remind you of two things. First, God is not like your human father, who abandoned you. God will never abandon or forsake you. He loves you with an infinite love! Believe in that love and respond to it generously.

Second, life is a gift from God. The gift is not restricted to this earthly life. God invites us to experience the fullness of life with him in heaven for all eternity.

How does faith prepare us for death? Faith paves the way to eternal life. But faith has to be linked to hope and hope to love. In the end, only eternal love remains. In the end, we will be judged on love.

Michael, know that I will pray for you and your return to the faith.

Your sister in Christ,
Sister Mary Grace Donnellan

Michael folded the letter and put it in his pocket. He put his head down on his desk and closed his eyes in prayer. He prayed for the first time in a very long time. Warmth seemed to re-enter his body and life re-entered his soul.

The sound of his telephone ringing startled Michael, as if he were being roused from a deep sleep.

"Hello, this is Professor Reid."

"Professor Reid, this is Sister Mary Rose from Immaculate Heart of Mary Convent. I am calling to inform you of the death of Sister Mary Grace Donnellan. You had an appointment to interview her tomorrow."

"Didn't we just talk?"

"Pardon? I've never spoken to you before, Professor."

"Ah, it must have been someone else. Well, thank you for calling me. Please extend my condolences to her niece."

Michael ran his hands through his hair and wondered what had just occurred. Did he fall asleep? Was his interview with Sister Mary Grace nothing more than a dream? Then suddenly he reached for the tape recorder. He rewound the tape. Pressing the start button, he heard nothing back. He reached into his pocket, remembering the note that Sister Mary Grace had written.

Instead of a note, he found a fortune cookie. The curious thing was that he had not eaten in a Chinese restaurant for weeks, and he didn't remember taking a fortune cookie.

Breaking the cookie open, he unrolled the paper. His fortune read: "HE WHO HAS FAITH LIVES FOREVER." Michael laughed out loud. Whatever occurred was something supernatural, he was positive about that.

Then he opened his file folder on Sister Mary Grace Donnellan. In it was a sealed brown envelope that Beth Donnellan had given to him regarding her aunt. He unsealed the envelope and found Sister Mary Grace's curriculum vitae. His eyes opened wide when he saw a photo of her. She wore a blue habit and black veil. Her face was very familiar!

Michael folded his hands in prayer and poured out his soul to God. He promised God that he would make amends for the damage he had done to his students through the years. Rebecca, the freshman from his Sociology of Religion course, would be the first student to whom he would speak with about his faith.

He thumbed through the index cards he had on his students. He found Rebecca's cell phone number. Beneath this information, she had written the following statement regarding her expectations for the course she was taking with Professor Reid.

"I am hoping that this Sociology of Religion course will help me to understand how God influences our lives as individuals, in groups and in society as a whole."

Paul dialed Rebecca's cell phone number, hoping she would respond.

"Hello."

"Rebecca, Becky. This is Professor Reid. I hope I haven't called at an inconvenient time."

"Not at all!"

"Becky, I want to apologize for my behavior earlier today. My comments to you about my beliefs misrepresented the truth. I would like to speak to you about my faith. I do believe in God. I'll explain when I see you."

Becky made arrangements to meet with her professor later that afternoon.

"You don't know how much this means to me, Professor Reid!"

"I think I do," he told her.

CHAPTER 41
DENISE SMITH
AND BRENDA HERMANN

Now there was a man of the Pharisees, named Nicode-mus, a ruler of the Jews. This man came to Jesus by night and said to him, "Rabbi, we know that you are a teacher come from God; for no one can do these signs that you do, unless God is with him." Jesus answered him, "Truly, truly, I say to you, unless one is born anew, he cannot see the kingdom of God." Nicodemus said to him, "How can a man be born when he is old? Can he enter a second time into his mother's womb and be born?" Jesus answered, "Truly, truly, I say to you, unless one is born of water and the Spirit, he cannot enter the kingdom of God. That which is born of the flesh is flesh, and that which is born of the Spirit is spirit."

(John 3:1–6)

Denise was emotionally exhausted. She and her parents had returned home from the hospital and decided it was best to delay any serious discussions about her pregnancy. What was clear was that Denise would have the baby.

"Go to bed, honey. There's nothing more you can do for Brenda tonight," Denise's mother said.

Denise shook her head in agreement. As she closed the door of her bedroom, she began to sob.

"Brenda, please don't die!"

Sitting on her bed, she again picked up her stuffed bear named Barnie. Her mind returned to her childhood. She and Brenda had gone to school together through high school. What surprised Denise was the fact that Brenda had never been baptized, though both of her parents considered themselves Christians.

When Denise was being prepared for First Communion, Brenda sat through all the classes at All Saints School. It was clear to Denise that Brenda believed in the Real Presence of Jesus in the Eucharist. Actually, she believed everything she was taught on the faith in their twelve years of Catholic education.

Denise remembered a conversation they had when they were in the seventh grade.

"Brenda, why don't you ask your parents if you can become Catholic?"

"Denise, my parents say that I can't convert until my eighteenth birthday. They don't want our friendship to influence my decision."

Suddenly, Denise's cell phone began to ring.

"Hello, Mrs. Hermann. What do you mean, there's little hope? I'll be back at the hospital in 20 minutes!"

Denise decided not to tell her parents she was returning to the hospital. She scribbled a note to them and quickly left the house.

As Denise drove to the hospital, she prayed that she would be in time to comfort her friend.

Denise walked into ICU and approached the nurse.

"Brenda's parents called me. They said Brenda is dying."

The nurse looked up, realizing that Denise had been crying.

"There's not much you can do for her."

Denise held back the tears.

"Where are her parents?"

"Mrs. Hermann needed to rest. The doctor gave her a sedative. They're in the lounge if you want to see them."

"No, I need to see Brenda first."

"She slips in and out of consciousness. She may or may not know you are with her."

Denise indicated that she understood. As she stood by Brenda's bedside, Denise realized that the rosary she had placed in her friend's hand was lying beside her on the bed. She scooped it up and wrapped it around Brenda's wrist.

"Brenda, don't give up! Please don't give up! I believe you can hear me."

Taking Brenda's free hand, she held it.

"If you can hear me, try to squeeze my hand."

Denise felt her friend's attempt to let her know she was aware of her presence.

"Brenda, are you alone? Squeeze once for yes and twice for no."

Denise waited. It seemed like an eternity. Suddenly, she felt Brenda squeeze her hand twice.

"That creature is with her!" thought Denise.

Brenda remained silent.

"She can't help you, pumpkin. It's kind of funny. She was going to have the abortion and you're the one who is dying and going to hell!"

Denise drew close to Brenda. Speaking into her friend's ear, she said, "Brenda, listen carefully to me. I want to baptize you. You were never baptized. You couldn't choose in seventh grade, but you certainly can choose now. Do you want to be baptized, Brenda? Squeeze my hand once if you want to be baptized and twice if you don't."

Denise waited and waited. She prayed that Brenda would ask for baptism.

Satan watched as Brenda looked down at her hand.

"What are you thinking, my little pumpkin?"

Brenda could hear Denise's voice. She heard something about baptism, but couldn't hear the question. Satan's loud laughs and taunts distracted her.

"Brenda, I'm not going to give up! Tell me if you want to be baptized. Squeeze once if you want baptism."

Brenda heard her this time. Denise felt Brenda squeeze her hand once very firmly.

"O.K.!"

Satan began to swear.

"Look down into the abyss, Brenda. That's where you are going. Forget Denise and her superstitious nonsense. You are mine!"

Brenda yelled, "No! No! I am not yours! Oh, Jesus, help me!"

Satan was startled by Brenda's refusal to submit to him.

"Don't get me angry, pumpkin."

With a thought, he flung her against the cave wall. She landed face down. Instead of rising, she clasped her hands together, in prayer, as she lay prostrate.

"You disgust me," Satan screamed.

Brenda could hear Denise's voice.

"Brenda, I know you understand what baptism is all about. Desire it with all your heart!"

Brenda concentrated in prayer, "Lord, I want to be reborn. I desire the waters of baptism. Free me from all sin. Free me from Satan . . ."

Denise reached into her bag for the plastic bottle of blessed water she had placed there earlier in the evening. Pouring the holy water on Brenda's forehead three times, she said, "I baptize you, Brenda Mary, in the name of the Father, and of the Son, and of the Holy Spirit."

Brenda responded from the pit.

"Amen."

She felt something cool trickle down her face. It was the very waters of baptism.

Satan screamed and howled like an animal. His angry outburst faded into nothingness as Brenda opened her eyes and looked into Denise's face.

Unable to speak, she simply smiled at Denise.

The nurse came into the room.

"Her eyes are open," declared Denise.

"I can see that. The doctor is on his way. We've been monitoring her."

As Denise began to move away from the bed, she felt Brenda's hand holding on to her hand. She read the words "Thank you" Brenda's lips.

"Brenda, I'll be back."

With victory in her smile, Denise walked backward toward the door. "I'll be back!"

CHAPTER 42
NICK TROIANO

"Who then is the faithful and wise servant, whom his master has set over his household, to give them their food at the proper time? Blessed is that servant whom his master when he comes will find so doing. Truly, I say to you, he will set him over all his possessions. But if that wicked servant says to himself, 'My master is delayed,' and begins to beat his fellow servants, and eats and drinks with the drunken, the master of that servant will come on a day when he does not expect him and at an hour he does not know, and will punish him, and put him with the hypocrites; there men will weep and gnash their teeth."
(Matthew 24:45–51)

Nick Troiano found himself face to face with evil incarnate.

"I know you, don't I?" Nick asked with an air of arrogance.

"You sure do! We've been collaborators for years, Nicky. I was the brains behind all your operations. It didn't take much to motivate you."

"What? No one tells me what to do!"

"Really?"

"Yeah, really."

"So who the hell are you? Where's that jerk, Larry?"

"Your dear friend is gone forever. Did you know he despised you? I thought I had him on the hook. Unfortunately, Larry had a last-minute conversion. I hate those final few seconds when people can flee from me! Now, you, Nicky, you never tried to flee me. Oh, sure there were a few rare moments through the years when you had second thoughts about your life of crime. You felt drawn to goodness. You had me worried a few years back when you were talking to your wife about wanting to reform your life. Thankfully, nothing overly significant followed that heartwarming confession to your pretty little Lisa. Nicky, you're one of the gang!"

Nick hated the fact that Satan even referred to his wife in the conversation.

Satan continued, "On Earth you were a gangster, a crime boss, a capo. You and some of the members of your family wreaked havoc in Queens and Brooklyn for years! You thrived on money, power, pleasure and influence. And like Frank Sinatra sang years ago, 'You did it your way.' The Troiano crime family, however, will pass into oblivion in a few years. But here, in my kingdom, Nicky, you and your past will live on forever in infamy. You're part of the gang."

"But why do you call this a 'gang'?"

"We are Legion, for we are many. Here, I am the head, the capo. Everyone does as I say, as I command."

"What's in it for me?"

"Oh, you get to reign with Legion. Think of the possibilities! You can influence political races, governments, empires, even the stock market. The world is filled with weak creatures that need to be controlled by Legion. Power, my friend, it's about exercising brute power."

Nick enjoyed the conversation that followed about controlling the world. He delighted in the idea that he could be instrumental in fashioning human history. The discussion with Satan was intoxicating, stimulating and extremely pleasurable.

Then Nick did the unspeakable. He moved toward Satan and put his arm around his shoulders. As he did this, Satan emitted a dreadful odor. It was so nauseating that Nick had to move away from the vile creature.

"Let's get something straight, you despicable little man. We are not pals. I am your master and you are my slave."

Nick straightened up. The handsome human face he had been looking at was now anything but handsome. His appearance instilled only fear and repugnance in Nick. Satan looked more like an animal than a man. His eyes were lifeless and black, surrounded by red. His mouth revealed razor-like teeth and a serpent-like tongue. Even his hands revealed claw-like nails that could strip flesh off the human body.

"You owe me homage, Nicky. Get down on your miserable little knees and pay me homage or I'll strip the skin from your body with my bare hands."

Nick dropped to his knees and bowed before Satan. He trembled with fear.

"Now, that's better, Nicky. Don't forget your place in my kingdom. I can reward you for your actions, but I can also punish you. Punishment in hell is eternal, you know. Don't doubt that you can feel pain."

Satan proceeded to slash Nick's face with his claws. Nick screamed in agony. The flesh from his cheek was torn open and his face was bleeding profusely. Satan roared with laughter.

"This is your first lesson in obedience. Don't ever cross me. Remember, I can make your life a living hell!"

Satan roared with laughter again. Nicky could hear the demons laughing with him in the background.

"Laugh, Nicky! Let me hear you laugh! Don't stop until I tell you."

Nick began to laugh out loud.

"No, Nicky, louder, louder. Laugh, you fool!"

Out of fear, Nick laughed with all his might. As he did so, tears of desperation ran down his cheeks. The tears that flowed from his eyes were like acid on his cheeks, burning through his raw and bloody flesh. The tears ate

Nick's eyes until they were consumed and he was totally blinded.

"Laugh, Nicky. Keep laughing. The joke is on you!"

Nick began to scream, curse and yell out profanities. Yet, all the time, he continued laughing.

"Good, Nicky. Keep it up. Don't stop!"

Nick could not move from the spot where he was kneeling. Blinded, burning alive from his own tears, he felt only hatred, desperation and desire to escape his captor.

Moments passed. Nick's face beneath his eyes was eaten away to the bone. He could no longer laugh, scream, curse or yell out profanities. The darkness, pain and agony were beyond anything he could have imagined in his life. What caused him the greatest agony was the realization that there was no escape, no relief, no way out for him.

"Get up, you filthy pig. Get up on your feet."

Nick stood up, unable to see or speak.

"I will restore your ugly face. Then I will send you to do my bidding in the world. Do you understand?"

As Satan asked this question, he restored Nick's face.

"Yes, Master. Whatever you say."

"You'll start with the Catholic politicians, Nicky. Did you know most of them are personally opposed to abortion? I absolutely applauded the arrogance of that Catholic governor from the East Coast who delivered a speech on the legitimacy of the pro-choice position at a prestigious Catholic University years ago. I can't wait for him to join me! He's going to listen to his brilliant speech for all eternity! Don't you think that will be a great tribute to him, Nicky?"

"Yes, Master."

"I want you to work with Legion on keeping the Catholic politicians on the right course of action. They must grow in their pride, arrogance and disobedience. And yes, I want more of them to receive sacrilegious Communions. I love that "in your face" attitude they have toward the Church and my archenemy. It is so inspirational! Don't you agree, Nicky?"

"Yes, Master."

"I want Planned Parenthood and all those pro-abortion groups to line the pockets of the politicians with money for their campaigns. Their election to political office must be assured. Oh, how my mind races . . . I want euthanasia, assisted suicide, embryonic stem-cell research, reproductive cloning, gay marriages and capital punishment to be legitimized and legalized."

"Yes, Master."

"Nicky, there is a movement in the United States to attack freedom of choice. Legion must oppose this movement vigorously. Find ways to undermine their strategies. Do you understand?"

"Yes, Master."

"Oh, Nicky, I have so many agendas in the world! When I want to entertain myself, I list all the evils in the world in alphabetical order. 'A' is for 'abortions, adultery, AIDS, the agenda of the American Civil Liberties Union and assaults by terrorists.' And 'B' is for 'bestiality, bigamy, black magic and brutality.' I could go and on . . . You know what my ultimate goal is, Nicky? I want to take with me as many despicable creatures like yourself that I can. Do you understand? I am the great seducer. I do my job extremely well."

"Yes, Master."

"In the name of all that is evil, I command you to join Legion in its mission to the world."

CHAPTER 43
NICK TROIANO

Lisa Troiano sat in the family room with her three children. The police had just arrived with the terrible news that Nick, his lawyer and the chauffeur were in a terrible accident on the Belt Parkway. Two of the passengers in the car were killed. One was still clinging to life.

"Is Daddy going to die?" asked little Nicky.

Lisa looked at her son, who so resembled her husband. As she thought about the possibility of her husband's death, she feared for him since he was not ready to meet God.

Lisa reached over to a framed photo on the lamp table. It was a picture from the previous Christmas. Nick had even agreed to accompany the family to midnight Mass, something he had never done before. Little Nicky had begged his father to join them. Nick could never resist the pleas of his children.

There were times that Nick seemed to be like any ordinary family man. He loved his children, and in his own peculiar way he loved his wife. Lisa recalled how distraught she was after learning that her husband had Mitch killed. For weeks, she remained cold and distant from her husband. Finally, one night, while she sat reading in the family room, Nick came to sit down beside her.

"Lisa, I know you think I'm an animal because you believe I had Mitch killed after Nicky's accident. I did not order that hit. That's the truth."

Lisa just stared at her husband.

"Babe, I didn't order that hit. I found out from Larry Klein that it was my stupid brother, Frank, who put a contract out on him. My brother saw how upset I was.

I think I said I wanted to kill Mitch for being so careless. Frank interpreted that as an order."

"Nick, how many other hits have you ordered? How many people have died because of your 'business?'"

Nick took his wife's hands into his own.

"Lisa, I'd give it all up for you and the kids if I could, but I'm in too deep now. If I could ever figure a way out, I promise you we would be out of here. I love you and the kids even more than my own life. Please believe me."

Lisa allowed her husband to embrace her.

"Lisa, I want you and the kids to go to Florida. Your parents need you. Go for a month or so. We can hire some tutors for the children. I'll fly down every weekend. I never want you to doubt that I love you."

Replacing the photo on the table, Lisa turned to her son.

"I don't know if your father is going to live. It was a very bad accident. We need to pray real hard for Daddy. He needs us more than ever."

The twins, Theresa and Anne, both 6 years old, chimed in, "Mommy, why don't we pray for Daddy right now! We know the Hail Mary by heart!"

"O.K. Let's recite the Hail Mary together."

Gathering her three children around her, they knelt down and began to pray together.

Nick opened his eyes. He was terrified at what he would see. What would Satan do now to torture him? But instead of Satan, he saw doctors and nurses working hard to save his life. He was unable to speak or move and was in extreme pain.

Realizing that he was not dead, and that he was not yet condemned to hell, Nick felt relieved.

"The internal bleeding is massive. It doesn't look good," one of the doctors said.

Nick could hear everything going on around him, but couldn't respond. He felt totally powerless and vulnerable for the first time in his adult life. Then his life passed before his eyes. It wasn't a pretty picture. Murder, robbery, embezzlements, bribery and drug trade were his claim to fame.

Contrasting such evil in his life, Nick pictured his three beautiful children and wife. No matter what he did, he could return to them and be loved unconditionally. They made him human.

"I don't want to spend eternity in hell!!"

The pain in Nick's chest became unbearable. Nick's gaze rested on a man standing next to one of the nurses. He, too, was a doctor. Or was he? Nick stared at him. It was Satan who stood there smiling maliciously at him.

"Nicky, Nicky, it's much too late for you! Don't tell me you have regrets about your life! Anyway, you're really not sorry for your sins. Be honest, now."

Nick realized that only he heard and saw Satan. How could he respond to this creature? It was true that he enjoyed the power he wielded as a capo, which was intoxicating. He had the world on a string. He wasn't overly sorry for anything he did.

"Nicky, that scene by the accident was only to instill in you respect for me. In your business, you had to do unpleasant things to make sure people would respect you. You see the power I have. I need your respect and your undivided loyalty. Surely you can understand that I was testing you."

Nick glanced over at an elderly priest who stood in the corner reciting some prayers.

"Ignore that fool, Nick. He has nothing to offer you. You haven't been to church since the day you were married and one Christmas Eve when your son begged you to go. Don't be a hypocrite. You think you're really material for heaven?"

Then, in the secret of Nick's heart, he heard the words, "Where there is life, there is hope."

Struggling to hold on to life, he struggled with the thought of death and damnation as well as life and glory.

"Nicky, heaven is not an option for you. Resign yourself to the inevitable."

"No, no."

"Abandon your foolish thinking. You are incapable of sincere repentance. Give it up and throw your lot in with me."

Nick felt confused.

"How can God forgive me for all the terrible things I've done in my life?"

Then he heard the same voice again.

"Where there is life, there is hope."

It didn't make a whole lot of sense to him, but the thought consoled him. The explosion of pain in his chest diverted his attention.

"He's gone," the doctor announced.

At that moment, the elderly white-haired priest, Father Patrick Murphy, approached the gurney with his hand raised in a blessing. Satan retreated into the corner momentarily.

Then, like an animal that stalks its prey, Satan returned to Nick's body and salivated over it as the last ounces of life left it.

The priest looked down at the lifeless body of the mobster known to people as Slick Nick.

"Nick, I pray you made your peace with God before you died."

The priest proceeded to recite Psalm 51.

"Have mercy on me, God, in your kindness.
In your compassion, blot out my offense.
O wash me more and more from my guilt
and cleanse me of my sin."

The room began to clear of the medical personnel. The IV was detached from Nick's arm and the emergency equipment was rolled away. There was stillness in the room.

The last nurse to leave the room turned to Father Murphy, a former Army chaplain.

"Father, I'm curious. Do you think someone like Nick Troiano can be saved?"

"Well, we believe that Christ died for all sinners. That includes Nick. We know for a fact that he was a notorious public sinner. What we don't know is whether or not he surrendered his soul to God in the final moments of his life. We believe that where there is life, there is always hope. Life is like a battlefield, and it's not over until it's over.

Father Murphy took a seat next to Nick's body. Resting his head in both hands, Father Murphy prayed silently. The door opened and Reverend Paul Smith appeared. He was one of the Protestant chaplains on the ecumenical pastoral staff of the hospital. Placing his hand on his colleague's shoulder, and knowing the reputation of Nick Troiano, he said with a hint of humor in his voice, "I'm glad he was one of yours!"

Father Murphy turned to the Reverend Smith and smiled. Then he asked with all seriousness, "How long do you figure it takes the soul to leave the body when someone dies?

"That's a good question! Why? Do you sense that Nick is still with us?"

"I don't know. I just feel the need to remain with him a little longer."

Reverend Smith's pager sounded. "Well, I guess there's no rest for the weary! I just finished speaking to the parents of a teenage daughter who committed suicide! They are beside themselves with grief."

Father Murphy looked up, "How *you* holding up?"

"It's been a tough day . . . I'll see you at the staff meeting later."

As the minister exited the room, a physician entered. His gaze focused on Nick. He laughed as he realized that neither the priest nor the minister were aware of his presence.

The doctor looked down at his own wristwatch. It had no hands. Bending over the body, he whispered something into Nick's ear. He waited. He whispered again. He waited. A third time, he whispered into Nick's ear. He looked up at the wall clock. It was three o'clock.

Satan stepped back from Nick's body. He paced back and forth like an animal of prey. He hissed and moaned. And then it was all over. Nick had made the final choice. In eternity, his fate was sealed. He had thrown himself on the throne of divine mercy!

Satan turned to the priest, who was oblivious to his evil presence. He cursed. As Father Murphy concluded his prayers, Satan reeled in agony.

"Eternal God, in whom mercy is endless, and the treasury of compassion inexhaustible, look kindly upon us, and increase your Mercy in us, that in difficult moments, we might not despair, nor become despondent, but with great confidence, submit ourselves to your holy will, which is Love and Mercy itself. Amen."

As the priest left the room, it filled with demons and hideous creatures of the underworld. Satan screamed obscenities and blasphemies. Then suddenly he quieted down. He raised his head and walked to the doorway.

A broad smile appeared on Satan's face. He looked up and laughed.

Turning to the demons, he shouted, "I have a victory coming in! Join me in celebration!"

Satan and the demons left the room. They floated down the hospital corridor and congregated around the body of a beautiful young woman who had been involved in a car crash. She was near death.

Turning to the demons that encircled her body, Satan indicated that she was a famous actress and singer.

She was on her way to Kennedy Airport when her car collided with a minivan. She was famous for her lewd performances, and was preparing to tour the country. Satan was laughing.

"Let the entertainment begin!"

CHAPTER 44
BRENDA HERMANN AND DENISE SMITH

For with thee is the fountain of life; in thy light do we see light.

(Psalm 36:9)

Brenda's condition continued to improve. Her parents were coaxed into going home for a few hours of rest, comforted in the knowledge that Denise would remain with their daughter.

Brenda looked up at Denise.

"Who would believe what you and I experienced? Will he return? I mean, he must be very angry!"

"I know he's angry. And, yes, he will return, but not in such a dramatic way, at least I hope not. But we'll know when he returns because he will lie to us and tell us that we can sin without punishment, without consequences. Don't you think you will recognize his conniving voice?"

"But he could be subtle at times."

"The Church knows him as the father of lies. If we listen to the Church, even his subtle words will ring false in our ears."

"What was the experience like for you, Denise?"

Denise began to describe her vivid dream with all its horror and how she had even confessed her sins to Father Kassebart.

"You know, a dream or a nightmare originates in sleep. Think about this, sleep and death are similar experiences. Perhaps God permitted me a few seconds in a death-like sleep in order to help save me. Satan, who is not all-knowing, may not have been aware that I was asleep. He may have thought I was really dead! I suppose the joke was on him!"

Denise and Brenda laughed at the notion that Satan was the most foolish creature in the universe.

"Oh, Brendy, I'm so glad we made it out of our nightmares in one piece!"

Then a look of seriousness came over Brenda's face.

"You haven't called me 'Brendy' since our freshman year in high school. I told you then that I didn't like it because it made me sound like a nerd."

"I'm sorry, Brenda."

"No, don't be sorry. I like the sound of it again. Denise, right after you baptized me, and immediately before I opened my eyes, I returned to my bed and found myself floating down a long corridor. A young boy, around 6 years old, took hold of my hand. He was so cute. He looked a lot like you, when you were that age. He said to me, 'Brendy, don't be afraid. Follow me out.' It all happened in a split second, though it must have been longer."

"I think it was Joshua, my little brother who my mother miscarried when I was 6. I guess since you've always been like a sister to me, he figured he should be a good brother to you!"

Denise and Brenda spent the next hour talking, praying and dreaming of their futures that were firmly placed in God's hands.

Chapter 45
Father Patrick Murphy

Give ear to my words, O Lord; give heed to my groaning. Hearken to the sound of my cry, my King and my God, for to thee do I pray. O Lord, in the morning thou dost hear my voice; in the morning I prepare a sacrifice for thee, and watch. For thou art not a God who delights in wickedness; evil may not sojourn with thee.

(Psalm 5:1–4)

As Father Murphy left the room where Nick's body lay, he was alerted to the fact that an ambulance had brought in Emma Donnan, a famous actress and singer.

Satan and his minions were dancing around her body while making indecent gestures that the actress and singer had used in her performances. Then Satan emitted a loud guttural sound followed by inhuman screams. He cursed as he watched the good Father Murphy walk to her side.

The nurse turned to the priest, "Father, I don't think she's one of your flock. If she ever was, she's probably renounced her faith."

Without looking at the nurse, Father Murphy replied, "That's O.K. I'll pray for her anyway."

In silence, Father Murphy prayed, "Go forth from this world, O Christian soul, in the name of God who created you . . ."

The woman was pronounced dead as she made the final choice.

As Father Murphy began to close his prayer book, a young nurse standing near the elderly priest said, "Father, I've always wondered how an all-merciful God can allow people to choose hell. It doesn't make sense!"

Father Murphy glanced at the nurse's nametag.

"Sheila, you're new here."

"Yes, I started a week ago."

"Well, Sheila, I noticed that you're wearing a wedding band. How long have you been married?"

Sheila smiled and replied, "Only six months."

"What's your husband's name?"

"Tim."

"Do you love Tim?"

Sheila looked at the priest with a puzzled expression.

"Of course, I love him. If I didn't, I wouldn't have married him."

"Does Tim love you?"

"Of course! Why all these questions?"

"Bear with me. Try to imagine, for a minute, the possibility that Tim had no other choice but to love you. How does that strike you?"

"Well, if he had no choice but to love me then could that really be love? He chose me to be his wife because he loved me."

"Exactly. Love is selective, it seeks out, it chooses. God will not force us to love him. God wants us to select him, to seek him out, to choose him. God is merciful, very merciful. In his mercy, he calls sinners back to himself. He bathes them in his merciful love and forgiveness when they turn to him. But he will not destroy our free will. Free will is a gift from our Creator. Unlike other creatures or lower forms of life, we possess this gift that makes us like God."

"It's frightening to think that we can choose freely to reject God and not love him."

Father Murphy shook his head in agreement.

"Yes, it is a most frightening reality. It should be a sobering reality for all of us."

Then, glancing at the body of Emma Donnan, Father Murphy thought to himself, "Emma, I hope you exercised your free will to choose God."

Part III—The Path to Life

CHAPTER 46
FIVE YEARS LATER—THE WEDDING

Let us test and examine our ways, and return to the Lord!

(Lamentations 3:40)

Brenda Hermann looked radiant in her wedding gown. All Saints Church was filled with relatives and friends. Her strawberry blond hair was pulled back from her face and fell in waves of curls under her veil. She kept dabbing powder on her face to hide her freckles.

"Oh, Brenda, Gary loves your freckles. Stop fussing," Denise said as she hugged her best friend.

"Aunt Brendy, can you fix my tie?" little Jesse asked with an impatient tone. "I'm not used to these clothes. When can I take them off?"

"Hopefully not until after the wedding reception, Jesse! Here, let me fix that tie for you."

She glanced at Denise with a look that only the two of them understood. Denise's son was the spitting image of Joshua, her baby brother.

"Denise, I can't wait to serve as your matron of honor in a few months when you marry Michael."

Though both couples had considered a double ceremony, Denise and Michael had opted for a wedding date closer to the Solemnity of the Immaculate Conception.

Denise smiled, knowing that both of them had been blessed with wonderful men with whom to spend the rest of their lives.

Professor Michael Reid, who had just turned 36 years old, was her soul mate. They had met by accident in Central Park while he was riding his bicycle. He had nearly plowed down Denise and Jesse, and apologized profusely for his carelessness.

Michael and Denise began to talk as they watched Jesse play, and in turn played with him. Within hours, a relationship was budding. In the weeks and months that followed, Denise delighted in watching Michael and Jesse grow close. His marriage proposal was no surprise; they knew they were made for each other.

"You know, Denise, starting with a family is kind of nice," Michael said. "Five years ago, I would have laughed at anyone who told me that I would be a married man and raising a child! It's funny how God can open your mind and heart to his way of thinking."

Denise added, "And to his way of loving."

She was jolted back to the present moment.

"Denise, you're a thousand miles away," said Brenda.

Denise adjusted her lilac-colored chiffon gown and repositioned her wide-brimmed straw hat. Then she took Brenda's arm.

"Just reminiscing. Are you nervous, kid?"

"A little, but I'm more excited than nervous."

Brenda thought of her husband-to-be, Gary Thomas, a certified public accountant from Long Island. He was everything she wanted in a husband. He was intelligent, thoughtful, kind, considerate, and had a great sense of humor.

His sister, Lisa Thomas Troiano, found him to be the ideal uncle for her children. When they lost their father so tragically, Gary had stepped in as a surrogate father and his positive influence in their lives was paying off. Though Nick's brothers still visited the children, it was obvious that the values of the Thomas family were taking root in the Troiano children.

Lisa Troiano and her children were seated in one of the first pews. Turning to his mother and tapping her on the arm, Nicky whispered, "Mom, if Dad did so many bad things in his life, why did you marry him in the first place?"

Lisa hesitated a moment. Her mind drifted back to her own wedding at St. Augustine Church. Nick was waiting at the altar as she began to walk down the aisle with her father. Nick looked back at her and smiled. By that time, she was well aware of his family's illegal enterprises and hoped against hope that he would find a way to be liberated from it all. She prayed that he would make T-Men Inc. into the thriving business he dreamed was possible.

Right before she and Nick turned to the priest to exchange their marriage vows, he whispered in her ear, "Never doubt my love for you, no matter what, never."

Lisa smiled at her son.

"Nicky, you remember your father, don't you?"

"Of course! We did a lot of neat things together."

"Well, did you love him?"

Nicky felt uncomfortable.

"Sure, I loved him. He was my father!"

"Well, I loved him because he was my husband. Your father had a dark side to his personality, but he also had the good side that he showed to you, to your sisters and to me. What you loved in him, I loved. Don't ever doubt that he loved us."

"Do you think he's with God or with the other guy? You know who I mean."

"Nicky, I pray that your father rejected the darkness in his life and chose to live in the light when he was dying."

Then she asked Nicky if he recalled the terrifying incident in Florida when he was 9 years old and swam out into deep water and developed a leg cramp. He had been warned to stay close to shore, but had disregarded his father's instructions.

As he began flailing his arms in the air, an alert lifeguard jumped in to save him. His father was right behind the lifeguard. Nicky was pulled to shore and placed on the sand. Although he had swallowed a great deal of water, he was otherwise fine. As he lay on the sand, he looked up at his father with fear because he had disobeyed him. Nick grabbed his son in his arms and hugged him. Without saying a word, he began massaging his son's leg.

"Mom, you were nearly hysterical. I kept telling you both that I was sorry. I thought I was going to be punished."

"And then what did you father say and do?"

Nicky looked at his mother, shaking his head up and down.

"He said, 'Nicky, if you had drowned, I don't know what I would have done. I love you. Please, son, listen to me when I tell you not to do something.'"

"Then he picked you up in his arms and carried you to our blanket, kissing you as he put you down. Your father loved you, Nicky. We know that God the Father's love far surpasses the love of a human father. I believe that when your father was dying, God brought him close to his heart and gave him a last chance at repentance. I believe your father would have returned the embrace of God like the prodigal son in the Bible."

Nicky turned around in his seat and smiled. He wanted to believe that his father was saved.

PART IV—THE PATH PURSUED

CHAPTER 47

Now the tax collectors and sinners were all drawing near to hear him. And the Pharisees and the scribes murmured, saying, "This man receives sinners and eats with them." So he told them this parable: "What man of you, having a hundred sheep, if he has lost one of them, does not leave the ninety-nine in the wilderness, and go after the one which is lost, until he finds it? And when he has found it, he lays it on his shoulders, rejoicing. And when he comes home, he calls together his friends and his neighbors, saying to them, 'Rejoice with me, for I have found my sheep which was lost.' Just so, I tell you, there will be more joy in heaven over one sinner who repents than over ninety-nine righteous persons who need no repentance."
(Luke 15:1–7)

Denise adjusted Brenda's train.

"Why the sad look on your face, Denise?"

"Oh, I was just thinking that now that you and Gary are moving to Westchester, Michael and I won't be able to visit you as often. I suppose we can always talk on the phone . . ."

"I have a secret!"

Denise knew Brenda so well. As children she could always count on Brenda not to be able to keep a secret.

"Brenda, what secret do you have? Come on now! You know you're dying to tell me!"

Without delay, Brenda proceeded to tell Denise that Ethel Weiss, a well-know philanthropist who had been in the papers recently for donating 1.5 million dollars to the ALS Foundation, had agreed to sell her Westchester house to Brenda and Gary for a very reasonable price. When she heard they were getting married and looking forward to having a large family, Ethel instantly decided that her home was to become their home.

Brenda recalled that Ethel shared with them that she was a pediatric nurse and loved children. She had one daughter who died tragically in a hit-and-run accident, and was unable to bring other pregnancies to term.

"I had one miscarriage after another," Ethel told her. "Maybe today with all the advancements, I could have had another child. But maybe doesn't count . . ."

Ethel went on to tell Brenda about her husband, who had been a physician. She omitted the facts about his untimely death and his involvement in the abortion industry. There was no reason to share this tragic piece of information. Anyway, she wanted to honor her late husband by remembering his achievements rather than his failures in life.

Ethel went on to tell Brenda and Gary that her longtime next-door neighbors, Martin and Barbara Fletcher, were also ready to put their house up for sale. Gary had passed on the information to Michael, who in turn made some initial contacts with the Fletchers.

"Denise, Michael is taking you house-hunting this weekend. Guess where the first stop will be!"

"You never could keep a secret, Brenda!"

"And aren't you glad about that!"

They both laughed like silly schoolgirls.

Denise peeked out into the congregation. She saw Michael sitting in a pew, looking extremely pensive.

"I wonder if he is thinking about our wedding day?"

Michael's eyes were fixed on the statue of the Blessed Mother on the side altar. As he considered his upcoming marriage to Denise, he couldn't help but think about Sister Mary Grace. He realized that his extraordinary experience had played a pivotal role in bringing him to faith. His faith led him to many positive experiences, which led him to Denise and Jesse. In the silence of his heart, he uttered a prayer of thanksgiving then recited a Hail, Mary for Sister Mary Grace.

He recalled that after his telephone conversation with Sister Mary Grace's superior, he had decided to attend her wake service and Mass. He entered the parlor of the convent and could see Sister Mary Grace's body in her casket. As he knelt down by the coffin, he looked at her body. It was indeed the woman he had encountered in his office the day before.

"Sister Mary Grace, thank you for making a pit stop to visit me the other day. You must have been a very effective teacher in life because you certainly taught me a thing or two."

Michael made the sign of the cross and went over to talk with Beth Donnellan, Sister Mary Grace's grandniece.

"Your aunt was quite a remarkable woman."

Beth smiled.

"When did you meet her?"

Michael realized that he made a slip.

"Actually, I would have loved to have met her before her death. I understand that she was quite an amazing woman."

"She was an extraordinary woman. One of the last things she said to me was that she intended to talk to you if it was the last thing she did. I have to admit that I told her you were an atheist. She was determined to shake you up and knock some sense into you. I'm sorry you never met her.

Michael laughed then proceeded to tell Beth that his thoughts about God had evolved since his last class.

Not wanting to monopolize Beth's time, he concluded, "I look forward to seeing you in my next class. Again, my condolences."

As he left the parlor, he turned one last time to glance at Sister Mary Grace's body in the casket then he picked up the prayer card with her photograph. He turned it over and read the quote from Scripture that she had selected. Later on, he learned from Beth that it was her aunt's favorite Bible passage:

For I am sure that neither death, nor life, nor angels, nor principalities, nor things present, nor things to come, nor powers, nor height, nor depth, nor anything else in all creation, will be able to separate us from the love of God in Christ Jesus our Lord. (Romans 8:38–39)

CHAPTER 48
THE LOVING THAT GIVES LIFE

*Praise the Lord! Praise the Lord, O my soul! I will praise
the Lord as long as I live; I will sing praises to my God
while I have being.*

(Psalm 146:1–2)

Shelley DeSimone picked up her single white
rose and stood with the other bridesmaids, who wore deep
pink chiffon gowns.

Turning to Brenda, she said, "This time I'd better catch the bouquet! I'd like to get married before my
thirty-fifth birthday!"

Shelley and Brenda were first cousins. Their
mothers, Rosemary and Kay Studzinsky, were sisters who
grew up on the north shore of Long Island.

While Kay and George Hermann opened a restaurant specializing in German and Polish cuisine in
Brooklyn, Rosemary and John DeSimone relocated to the
Midwest, where John, a chemist, found employment in
pharmaceutical research with Lally Drugs in Indianapolis. Despite the distance, Shelley and her cousins enjoyed
yearly visits that bonded them for life.

After Shelley's suicide attempt, the doctors determined that she was no longer a threat to herself and
released her from the hospital in record time. She returned
to her everyday activities with a new sense of self and
purpose. She was at peace.

Mark Kramer and his wife had a baby girl. Three
years later, they added a second daughter to their family.

Not only had their marriage survived the trauma of infidelity, it had grown stronger.

Like Mark, Shelley had been given a second chance in her own life and the quality of her life improved dramatically. She began volunteering at St. Elizabeth's Home for unwed mothers on the south side of town. She would often help tutor the young moms-to-be and help them with their schoolwork.

A year after her suicide attempt, when she was 30 years old, Shelley decided to contact her biological mother. Through St. Elizabeth's, initial contacts were made and Amber Powell, now a 45-year-old mother with three sons, agreed to meet her daughter.

Amber and Shelley met at a gazebo in Garfield Park in Indianapolis on a pleasant spring day in May. As soon as Shelley saw Amber walking toward the gazebo, she knew the woman was her mother. They were both of medium height and build. She had her mother's auburn hair. On closer inspection, she noticed that her mother's eyes were brown. Her father had hazel eyes, according to Amber, who showed Shelley a photograph of him taken in high school. She noticed that she had his straight hair, while her mother's hair was wavy.

They sat down and talked about their lives for hours. Shelley wanted to know all about her extended family, and Amber wanted to know about Shelley's life with the DeSimones.

"I never forgot you, Shelley. You were always here," she said as she placed her hand over heart.

Shelley was interested in learning about her three stepbrothers, all of whom where in school. One of her stepbrothers was still in high school, while Amber's two oldest sons attended Butler University in Indianapolis. They were thinking of becoming lawyers!

Amber had married after high school and was a stay-at-home mom while raising her sons. Her husband operated a car dealership in Indianapolis. At age 42, she had decided to return to school because she was interested in becoming a paralegal.

"Must be in the genes," Shelley mused.

She was pleased to meet her biological mother, but was rather disappointed to learn that her father, Danny Pike, turned out to be a real loser. Amber described him as "an impulsive boy who never thought about the consequences of his actions."

Shelley silently noted that her life five years earlier had been dramatically affected by her impulsive behavior that led to some pretty disastrous consequences!

As far as Amber knew, Danny had moved out of Indianapolis after high school to "God knows where." He had never expressed a desire to enter into the discussion about Shelley's adoption. His daughter was not important to him, and he had wanted Amber to have an abortion.

After sharing their life stories, their triumphs and their failures, Shelly took hold of Amber's hands.

"Amber, I want to thank you for giving birth to me and allowing Rosemary and Matt DeSimone to adopt me. I had a very good life with them. I loved them so much, and I have missed them dearly since they passed away. I admire you for the courage and love you had to bring me into the world."

"Shelley, when I discovered I was pregnant, my whole world seemed to collapse. Danny, your father, turned to me and said, 'Just get an abortion.' Even my best friend told me that she would accompany me to the clinic."

Amber described how she had spent a sleepless night and then went to school.

"I knew a baby was growing inside of me. I went to one of my teachers and confided in her. She led me to St. Elizabeth's. A teacher, a social worker and even a priest—and I'm not Catholic—helped me to bring you into the world."

Her mother gave her the names of the three people who were instrumental in helping her make a life-giving choice.

"Please find them and thank them for us."

Shelley's thoughts were interrupted by organ music and she smiled at her cousin, Brenda, who looked beautiful in her wedding dress.

The priest had gestured for the procession to begin and the organist began playing the wedding march.

Brenda gathered her train and, together with her bridal party, began to walk down the aisle of All Saints Church, the same church she and Denise attended as children.

She turned and kissed her father, George, who had been a non-practicing Christian and who had prevented his daughter's baptism. However, he was present for her full initiation into the faith that Easter following her accident.

Kay Studinsky Hermann, a fallen-away Catholic, also made her peace with the Lord shortly following her daughter's ordeal and near-death experience.

The bride-to-be began to walk slowly down the aisle. Holding her bouquet of white roses, she looked beyond Gary, who was beaming, and beyond the priest on the altar then fixed her gaze on the tabernacle and on Jesus, who was hidden in the tabernacle. She uttered a prayer of thanksgiving.

Without trying to look conspicuous, Denise searched the congregation for Mrs. Fitzpatrick. Though close to 80 years old, she still looked like a million bucks. Spotting her a few pews ahead, Denise smiled. Mrs. Fitzpatrick pulled her dainty handkerchief from her purse and dabbed at her nose as she watched her two former students, Denise and Brenda, moving gracefully down the aisle. Mrs. Fitzpatrick always cried at weddings, funerals and at the end of a good story.

Mrs. Fitzpatrick reached over to Pat Marino Lutz as she struggled to keep her toddler under control.

"Here, let me have that little angel," she said as she gathered the squirming child in her arms.

Pat handed over her fidgety child to the experienced Mrs. Fitzpatrick.

Like Denise and Brenda, Pat also found a man with whom to build a solid marriage. Brian Lutz and Pat Marino were classmates from the first-grade through the eighth-grade at All Saints School. Brian, like so many of the children in her neighborhood, had the privilege of being a student in Mrs. Fitz' fourth grade classroom.

When Pat returned to the practice of her faith, she often went to Mass with Mrs. Fitz at Immaculate Heart of Mary Church, where she met Brian Lutz, a resident at St. John's Hospital in New York City. Mrs. Fitz reintroduced the two of them to each other and within a year they were married. Marie Angela was the spitting image of her father. She had ash blonde hair and big brown eyes with long lashes. She was 15 months old and a bundle of energy.

"Pat, your husband could never sit still in school. I have a feeling Marie Angela takes after her father!"

Pat simply raised her eyes to heaven.

Each day, she hugged her daughter, Marie, and thought of Angela. One night in a dream, she saw Angela playing in a garden with other little children. She waved to Pat and threw her a kiss. Pat wanted to run to her daughter and scoop her curly redheaded baby into her arms. But there was a barrier between them. She knew the barrier was between life and death. As the dream ended, she could hear Angela reciting rhymes then clearly in her heart she heard these precious words:

"I Am who Am has set me free
to live and love and to be.
One day we'll meet again,
just you and me.

Remember, in his love,
I live eternally."

Pat was deeply consoled by these words and knew that her daughter was not only at peace, but also in the very embrace of Divine Love.

Two years earlier, Pat had participated in a post-abortion retreat experience then joined a post-abortion support group in her diocese. Always in the back of her mind, she thought about how she could help other post-abortive women. Shortly afterward, she decided to return to school and earned a master's degree in counseling, which she used as a therapist through Catholic Charities. She especially was committed to counseling post-abortive women, who were referred to her.

In her work, she recalled one woman in particular, named Beth, who had experienced an abortion while in her mid-twenties. She was the mother of two young children. Her husband had lost his job and the financial pressures led them to consider abortion. She resisted the idea at first, but went along with her husband's decision. She wanted to be at peace with her husband, and the pregnancy seemed to prevent that peace.

She recalled being very overprotective of her children while they were growing up. Somewhere in the back of her mind, she feared that God would take them and punish her for her sin of abortion. She began having dreams of a child calling out to her. She heard the cries, but could not locate the child. One day in confession, she admitted her sin to the priest. Despite being forgiven by the Lord, she never forgave herself. He urged her to go for counseling.

Pat led Beth down a path of hope. Week after week, they spoke about her decisions as a young wife and mother, and the decision that resulted in decades of guilt, shame, depression, anxiety and fear that God had really not forgiven her. One day, she invited Beth to spend a few hours in the evening in the presence of the Lord. She wanted her to picture her child with the Lord. The following week, Beth returned with a story that made Pat relive her own experience with Angela.

Beth told Pat that she pictured her baby, whom she named J.J. for John Joseph, playing with Jesus in a beautiful garden. Jesus was seated on a flat rock while J.J. rolled a big ball to him. J.J. was no more than 3 years old. He was delighted to play and ran back and forth to retrieve the ball that had been tossed to him by the Lord.

When her son tired of playing with the ball, he would go over to the Lord, who bounced him on his knee or picked him up high in the air. At other times, J.J. simply laughed as Jesus tickled him or carried him around the garden to look at the flowers and birds in the trees. She told Pat that she lost track of time as she imagined this garden scene. The beautiful grace that she received was at the end of her meditation when her son turned to her, waved and blew her a kiss. For the first time in twenty years, she felt a profound peace. She knew that it was only a meditation, but one that had a curative effect in her life.

"Beth, the abortion industry has destroyed so many lives and given grief to so many women and men. They sell abortion as though it were as harmless as whitening your teeth, but what it actually does is rob you of your child, your dignity and it destroys your spiritual life. Abortion is a dirty and deadly business."

Pat went on to tell Beth that the Lord brings good even out of evil because he is God. Human history attests to this reality.

"From your meditation, take back this one truth and hold on to it. Your child is safe with the Lord, who loves J.J. with an everlasting love."

Beth turned to Pat.

"I want women to know the truth about abortion. I want them to know that it's not the quick fix they think it will be. I've lived in torment for two decades because of my abortion. I want them to know the truth! We have to start telling the truth! They need to be warned."

Pat agreed. But would telling the truth be enough? Certainly, she had been taught the truth about abortion by her parents. She, in fact, wanted Paul's baby.

She hesitated at first, but then said to Beth, "It's not just the truth about abortion that women need to hear. They need to hear and accept the living truths of the Gospel. What the Church teaches, of course, is based on Gospel truths."

CHAPTER 49
A MOMENT IN TIME, FOREVER IN ETERNITY

"The sting of death is sin, and the power of sin is the law. But thanks be to God, who gives us the victory through our Lord Jesus Christ."

(1 Corinthians 15:56–57)

The Mass and exchange of wedding vows concluded within an hour. As husband and wife, Brenda and Gary walked jubilantly down the aisle toward the church doors. It was a beautiful sunny day in late September. The leaves were just beginning to change in color.

As Brenda looked at the crowd gathered to wish them well, her heart skipped a beat when she saw a finely dressed man standing across the street from the church. He smiled at her. She stared him down this time. Then she opened her heart in prayer and asked God to make her marriage fruitful and holy. As she prayed, the image of Satan disappeared.

Gary turned to Brenda with a concerned look.

"What's the matter, honey? You look like you've seen a ghost!"

Brenda smiled at Gary.

"No, not a ghost," she replied, then thought to herself, "It was nothing more than an old pest who needs to be resisted and despised for what he is and what he does."

"Are you O.K.?"

"I'm perfectly fine."

She smiled and raised her arm to wave to everyone.

Following Brenda's recovery from her accident, there were two other incidents in which she thought, for a few split seconds, that she saw Satan in a crowd, in a mirror or on a subway train. However, each time he appeared, he was further and further away from her. She knew this would be his last appearance.

The limousine driver opened the back door for the newly married couple. Before they could slip into the back seat, there was an abrupt reminder of the fragility of human life. An ambulance siren sounded its shrill cry. As everyone turned to look at the speeding vehicle, many people realized that life and death were separated by only a series of moments in time that passes swiftly.

Mrs. Fitzpatrick looked at the speeding ambulance. She made the sign of the cross and thought of her late husband, Donald Fitzpatrick. He was only 53 years old when he suffered an aneurysm. It was sudden and unexpected. As he lay unconscious on their bed, she called 911.

Though less than fifteen minutes passed before an ambulance arrived, it seemed like an eternity to Eileen Fitzpatrick and her children. Donald was placed on a stretcher as the medics asked numerous questions.

"No, he was healthy. No, he had no symptoms."

She proceeded to tell them that they went to bed by eleven o'clock and that when she awoke she noticed he was not moving. Normally, he was the first one up on Saturday morning. He would go outside to get the newspaper in their front yard then put the coffee on to brew. But now he was unresponsive to her. Her oldest daughter, Beverly, was still at home.

Eileen Fitzpatrick screamed for Beverly to call 911, which she did. The rest of the children stood around the bed, staring down at their father as he lay motionless. It was an unforgettable and dreadful moment in their lives.

Eileen remembered sitting in the ambulance feeling so helpless and alone. Her world was turned upside down without warning. Being a woman of faith, she turned to the Lord in prayer as the ambulance sped to the hospital. She had a sinking feeling that her husband was beyond her reach and the help of medicine.

The family gathered in the waiting area with Eileen and waited for the verdict. The doctor entered the room, removed his cap and invited the family to be seated. Then he delivered the dreaded news.

"Your husband passed on, Mrs. Fitzpatrick. He never regained consciousness."

Eileen Fitzpatrick and her children wept as the reality of their loss began to sink in. Again, she wept not as a woman who was desperate, but as a woman with faith.

Turning to her children, she told them, "He's with God now."

As the sound of the ambulance siren outside the church began to fade, she prayed silently, "Lord, guide that soul into your everlasting presence."

CHAPTER 50
GRANDMA PEARL, JAY ROKER
AND THE GUARDIAN ANGELS

Angels have been present since creation and throughout the history of salvation, announcing this salvation from afar or near and serving the accomplishment of the divine plan: they closed the earthly paradise; protected Lot; saved Hagar and her child; stayed Abraham's hand; communicated the law by their ministry; led the People of God; announced births and callings; assisted the prophets, just to cite a few examples. Finally, the angel Gabriel announced the birth of the Precursor and that of Jesus himself.
(Catechism of the Catholic Church, paragraph 332)

From its beginning until death, human life is surrounded by their watchful care and intercession. "Beside each believer stands an angel as protector and shepherd leading him to life." Already here on earth the Christian life shares by faith in the blessed company of angels and men united in God.
(Catechism of the Catholic Church, paragraph 336)

Jay Roker stood by the carousel as the children rode the wooden horses. The music was delightful, upbeat and soothing. The children looked around for familiar faces. Sometimes their guardian angels, who appeared as other children, would call out their names and wave to them. Some children immediately recognized family members or friends who awaited their arrival.

In some cases, the guardian angels ceded their privilege of accompanying the children to family members or friends during the first part of the journey to the Lord. The angels that did meet the children would introduce themselves to their particular child as they began to walk the path to the King.

Jay smiled as the children conversed with the angels and family members who greeted them. The children were of all ages, faiths and backgrounds. As they rode the carousel, they were being transformed, infused with knowledge about God without knowing it. They were responding to this knowledge with assent.

Children who had suffered from every known disease were riding the carousel. Some of the children were victims of violent crimes and murder victims. Some had died of illness or disease. Whatever the cause of their death, their well-being was restored with each turn of the carousel. Even the children who died from malnourishment began to appear healthy; their limbs no longer looked like sticks and took on flesh and muscle to allow them to walk and run.

Though the bodies of these children were spiritual bodies, they all knew that eventually they would have resurrected bodies. This knowledge was imparted to them on the carousel.

Jay was especially touched by the reactions of the children who were blind and began to see for the first time. They would cry out with such joy the second they could distinguish figures, colors, shapes and finally people. Their little hands would go to their eyes, and they would wipe the tears of joy away and laugh with pure delight.

Grandma Pearl stood next to Jay.

"This is what it's all about, Jay. Heaven is the fullness of life, the fullness of truth, the fullness of love."

Jay took his Grandma Pearl's hand and kissed it. They both smiled serenely as they watched the children transition into the next world.

Grandma Pearl continued to smile and placed her hand over her heart. She turned to her grandson whispered, "Samuel Weiss is crossing-over, Jay. He lived a life filled with so much sin and vice. Now he's coming into the fullness of life and the purifying rays of eternal light are penetrating his entire being. Praise our merciful and loving God!"

Grandma Pearl and Jay turned their attention back to the children, as they heard a 5-year-old boy from El Salvador who had been born blind, deaf and mute, cry out in Spanish, "I can see! I can hear! I can speak!"

The other children, from all the countries of the world, heard and understood his words. They all cried out in unison, "Thanks be to God!"

A 3-year-old Chinese girl hugged the neck of her wooden horse. Her parents had decided that they needed to have a male child, and because of China's one-child policy had abandoned her in the fields. A kind Christian woman found her and brought her to a state-run orphanage, where her life was barely sustained for three years. She knew no love, no hugs and no kisses, except from the Christian woman who reluctantly gave her up. The state would not permit her to keep this unwanted baby girl.

This child knew only the struggle to survive one day at a time. As she watched the other children on the carousel become healthy and strong, she also felt new surges of energy and wholeness run through her body. She glanced out at the crowd gathered around the carousel and saw a beautiful Chinese woman hold out her arms to her. She knew this woman was her great-grandmother.

Without using words, she heard the woman say, "I am here for you, Lily. I am here to love you."

Lily sat up on her horse.

"Will you hug me? Will you kiss me? Will you hold me?"

"Lily, I will love you always. In this kingdom, you will know only love! Come, my child, I have been waiting for you . . ."

The children dismounted and ran to their angels or family members or friends. After a few words, they accompanied their guides to the path leading to eternal life.

CHAPTER 51
CHRISTIAN KOHLER

"It is better for me to die in Christ Jesus than to reign over the ends of the earth. Him it is I seek–who died for us. Him it is I desire–who rose for us. I am on the point of giving birth. . . . Let me receive pure light; when I shall have arrived there, then shall I be a man."
(St. Ignatius of Antioch, Ad Rom., 6, 1–21)

Inside the ambulance that passed All Saints Church was a 4-year-old boy and his mother. He was dying of a rare form of cancer.

Anne Kohler sat beside her son in back of the ambulance.

"Oh God, please don't let my baby die."

Christian Kohler wasn't afraid to die. Actually, he didn't know what death really meant. What he did know was that his illness made his mother and father cry. As he lay in the ambulance, he could hear music, the kind that little children enjoy, and he smiled at his mother.

"Mommy, don't cry."

Anne looked down at her little boy. He was terribly pale and quite bald from the chemotherapy treatments he had just completed. She wiped the tears from her face.

"Oh, Chris, it's hard for Mommy not to cry. It hurts me to see you sick."

"Are they going to give me more treatments?"

"No, sweetheart. They finished with those."

"Good. I hate those treatments. I feel so tired."

Christian closed his eyes. As he did so, he heard the music getting louder. He almost forgot he was riding in an ambulance. It sounded like carousel music. He loved amusement parks and loved to go on the rides, especially the carousel.

Anne watched as her son lay motionless on the gurney. He looked as though he was asleep, but she knew he was slipping away from her. She glanced over at the medic, who was monitoring her son's vital signs. She could tell from the look on his face that her son was gone. She buried her face in her hands for a moment then stroked Chris' bald head and gently kissed his little hand.

The medic looked away from Anne. Though a medic for more than ten years, he could never really get used to the death of children.

Christian continued to listen to the carousel music. He imagined himself riding one of the colorful wooden horses going up and down. He imagined his parents standing by the carousel, smiling and waving to him as he passed them. Round and round he floated with the wooden horses.

The carousel was filled with other children enjoying the ride. He began to feel strength return to his little body. Slowly, the carousel came to a stop when the music ended. For a moment, Christian wondered how it was that he was riding a carousel since only minutes earlier he had been in an ambulance with his mother. He looked out in the crowd and saw a sea of little children. His parents were nowhere to be found.

"Christian, over here!" yelled a little girl about his age.

Standing next to her was a boy who was about 6 years old.

"Hi. My name's Joshua, but you can call me Josh. We came to bring you to the King."

Christian looked at the boy named Josh. He had light blonde hair and blue eyes.

"And my name is Angela. That's because the angels named me!"

Christian noticed her red curly hair and deep green eyes.

"Where are my Mommy and Daddy?"

"We were told to bring you to the King."

"But my Mommy is bringing me to the hospital to get better."

As Christian stood next to Joshua and Angela, he realized he no longer felt sick.

Angela giggled.

"Touch your head, Christian."

"Call me Chris, That's what everyone calls me."

Christian touched his head. His curly brown hair covered his entire head.

"Wow, I have hair again!!"

Joshua explained that Christian had passed from life on Earth to life in God's kingdom.

"Chris, the King sent us to bring you to him," Angela stated matter-of-factly.

"The King?"

Angela asked Christian if he knew who Jesus was.

Christian answered without hesitation, "God."

"That's right. Jesus is God. He's looking forward to seeing you. He wants you to be happy forever in his kingdom. Heaven is a place where the King lives. It's really a great place," Angela said with enthusiasm.

"Is it better than a toy store?"

Joshua and Angela laughed and shook their heads in agreement. Both chimed in, "Much better!"

They invited Christian to join them.

"Follow us and we'll take you to the King."

"But I'm sick."

"Not anymore," Josh said.

"But, what about my Mommy? Can't she come, too?"

"She's not ready to come. When it's her time to see the King, he'll send you to get her."

Christian began to follow his two new friends. He glanced around and saw children all around him.

"Are they going to see the King, too?"

Angela nodded.

As they walked away from the carousel, Christian noticed the trees, flowers and shrubbery around him.

"Gee, this is a pretty place!"

He was excited when he saw a few deer peeking out from the trees.

"Follow us, Chris," Josh said as he took Christian's hand.

Christian saw a beautiful river, sparkling clean. All kinds of people were gathered around the river and in it. Some of the adults were up to their waists in water.

"What are those people doing?" asked Christian.

"They are crossing-over into eternal life." Joshua said.

Christian wasn't sure what that meant.

Angela pointed to the path lined with all kinds of beautiful flowers.

"You see that path over there, Chris. That's the one the babies and children take to meet the King. Come on. We'll race you! Get on your mark, get set, go!!"

The three of them ran as fast as they could.

Christian won the race. He was amazed at the energy he possessed. He couldn't even walk five feet a few minutes ago.

"Well, Chris, you ran the race and the prize is yours!" Joshua said with firmness in his voice.

"I won! I won!" shouted Chris. "What's the prize?"

Joshua and Angela looked at each other and grinned.

"You'll see," they laughed.

The three of them began running down the path leading to the King of glory. Chris looked beneath his feet and saw rose petals of every color. He turned around, and

Josh and Angela were gone. Another little boy stood by his side.

"Hi. My name is Nathan. I'm your guardian angel."

"My guardian angel?"

Within a few seconds, Chris understood that this angel had been assigned to him when he came into existence in his mother's womb.

"I'm here to lead you to the King. But before you meet him, there is a beautiful woman, who is waiting for you."

"A beautiful woman? You mean my mommy?"

His angel smiled. Then he spoke to Chris' heart and revealed the true identity of the woman. Chris understood that she was the mother of Jesus Christ.

"Chris, there she is. Run to her!"

As his angel spoke, Chris saw Mary standing with her arms outstretched toward him. Her smile was so warm.

"Go ahead," Nathan urged him.

"Aren't you coming, too?"

"No. Mary will bring you into the presence of the King. I'll see you soon."

Delighted that he could run without effort, Christian ran toward the beautiful woman. As he did so, he kicked up rose petals.

Mary had a tender smile on her face. She gathered Christian in her arms, kissed him and told him he was a handsome little boy.

"I look like my Daddy."

"You sure do."

"Do you know my Daddy?"

"Oh, yes!"

"Christian, let me take you to my Son, Jesus. He loves you very much."

"And does he love my Mommy and Daddy?"

"Yes, Christian."

"Call me Chris."

Mary smiled.

"And does he love my Grandma Ellen and Grandpa Mike?"

"Yes."

"And does he love my beagle, Dexter?"

Mary's smile grew wider. As any other mother, she relished this dialogue with such an innocent child.

"Most definitely, Chris."

As he was about to name his goldfish and pet hamster, the Blessed Mother put her index finger over Christian's lips.

"He loves all of them very much!"

As Christian was carried in the arms of the Blessed Mother, she began to tell him all kinds of things about her Son and about her Son's kingdom.

"And I'll never be sick again?"

"That's right, Chris."

"Tell me more. Tell me more about Jesus and his kingdom."

"I'll do better than that, my child. I will place you in his very arms."

As Mary said this, they saw the Lord, in a long white flowing robe, walking toward them. He was smiling at Christian.

"That's Jesus! I have a picture of him in my room!"

Mary laughed sweetly. When Jesus was within an arm-length of them, Mary transferred Christian into her Son's arms.

"Are you the King?"

"I AM," said Jesus.

The Lord kissed Christian tenderly on his forehead. He began to whisper to him. Each time he whispered something to the child, Christian responded, "Ah ha."

Then Christian put both his arms around Jesus' neck and gave him the kind of hug he reserved for his father on Earth. They continued walking toward a great assembly of people all dressed in white. Christian was amazed at the number of people he saw there.

"Everyone is waiting for you, Chris. You'll never again be sick, afraid or alone. You will never again feel pain or sadness. You will be very happy here. You'll have so many friends forever."

Christian rubbed his little eyes. What he saw, what he heard and what he felt was beyond human words or expression. He opened his mouth in awe. Jesus again whispered something in his ear then placed Christian down and moved away from him.

Christian's eyes followed Jesus. Suddenly a bright light encircled him, a light brighter than he had ever seen. The light didn't hurt his eyes. He found himself within the circle of light and saw Jesus transfigured with the Father and the Holy Spirit. Christian dropped to his knees in adoration.

Then, with the wisdom of an adult, Christian said, "Lord, I am finally home."

TATE PUBLISHING, LLC

127 East Trade Center Terrace
Mustang, Oklahoma 73064

(888) 361 - 9473

TATE PUBLISHING, LLC
www.tatepublishing.com